EURO
HOW TO SAVE IT

By William Thayer

Author: William Thayer
Illustrator: Joan Boutselis

Table of Contents

Acronyms, Notes, Bibliography, Appendices

Why this book was written

Unless the Eurozone takes some of the necessary actions to curtail economic losses and encourage economic growth, I think the Euro will be greatly weakened and perhaps collapse. As an American, I suppose I could feel that this would just weaken a competitor to America. With the Euro greatly devalued and Eurozone economies in the gutter, America would be strengthened by comparison. However, I don't feel that way at all. I want the Euro to succeed and the Eurozone to be a strong, vibrant economic zone. The reason America entered both World War I (WWI) and World War II (WWII) was to help Europe be a force for the common good. The reason that America gave Europe aid after both WWI and WWII was that we wanted to see Europe prosper. After WWI, it was the Dawes and Young Plans. After WWII, it was the Marshall Plan.

My relatives fought in both wars. My grandfather, Lt. A.R. Thayer, served in WWI near Verdun. In WWII, Sgt. Kermit Glantz of the 17th Airborne Division fought in the relief of Bastogne and participated in the joint British-American parachute landings which help secure the crossing of the Rhine. From the American point of view, it seems we are always sending our young men to finish off European Civil Wars. We would far rather have the Europeans become united in mutual prosperity than be divided in the pursuit of Hegemonic Politics. *The Euro is important glue in uniting Europe and is worth saving for that reason alone.*

WWII Kermit Glantz [1]   WWI Lt. A.R. Thayer

In addition to my motivation to try and help the Eurozone, there is a second reason for this book. The European response to their crisis has been politically correct bailouts, politically correct bank stress tests (i.e., nearly everyone passes) and austerity budgets. The Eurozone needs some fresh thinking which this book will help to supply.

Finally, if "War is too important to left to Generals", then *"Economics is too important to be left to economists"*. Why? Well, just look at the results thus far on the Euro mess from the collection of economists and politicians directing the rescue effort. It includes "band aid" bailouts which just kick the can down the road. It includes the first bank stress test that indicated small Spanish banks needed help while the Irish banks are all right. Shortly after the results of the stress tests were announced, the Irish banks promptly proceeded to fail. What an incompetent stress test. Well, I don't come from the world of economics or politically correct politicians. I come from the world of logic and objectivity (science and engineering). With that advantage, I can supply some fresh thinking on the coming Euro Meltdown and how to avoid it.

Chapter 1. Executive Summary

The thesis of this book is that Greece and other PIG (Portugal, Ireland, Greece) countries will default on their debt, and the amount of financial damage caused by this will exceed the present $1 Trillion Eurozone bailout fund. The Eurozone must save the Euro by a combination of triage, pre-emption and growth. This book is divided into 5 Parts.

Part 1. Introduction
This Part will be an introduction to my modes of thinking which are quite different from the European Central Bank (ECB). The whole Eurozone problem is extremely complex. This book will approach the issues in a very simplified manner. Nevertheless, this simplified manner is more than what the ECB is doing. How well can a simplified approach work? Not too bad. In the middle of 2010, I wrote a simple book analyzing the causes of the Wall St. Panic of 2008. In February of 2011, the Financial Crisis Inquiry Commission Report on the same subject confirmed my major conclusions.

Part 2. Financial Death Spiral
This Part explains what is meant by a Financial Death Spiral. It is a deadly combination of a large National Debt and large Budget Deficits. This combination results in an ever increasing level of expense which is almost impossible to escape from. The usual result is Default on the National Debt.

Part 3. Derivatives
The Eurozone is facing a Financial Death Spiral for several of its members. Unfortunately, this is not the only problem it

faces. In the Wall St. Panic of 2008, Derivatives amplified the damage from the failure of Subprime Mortgages. It is likely that a similar effect will occur in the Eurozone. There are a variety of different types of Derivatives. It takes a ***different triggering event*** to explode each of these different Derivative Time Bombs. The trigger that will explode Derivatives relative to the Euro is a spike in interest rates. The ECB and financial media are not even discussing this issue. This book will.

Part 4. Growth

Parts 2 and 3 are grim forecasts. Am I a total pessimist? No. Basically, I am an optimist, but I believe there is a tremendous amount of mismanagement in our financial world (both governmental and private). The response to the PIG problems has been bailouts. This does not solve the underlying problems. It merely transfers them. What can solve these underlying problems? Growth. Growth can come from a combination of more work, real marketing and more innovation. We have tools that people couldn't even dream of 100 years ago. We are sitting on the threshold of the knowledge revolution that will transform this world for the better..... if we can get by our present financial problems.

Part 5. Summary

This part summarizes the basic themes of this book.

Chapter 2. Economics is too important

If war is too important to be left to generals, then ***"Economics is certainly too important to be left to economists"***. After reading this book, you will certainly see that I do not have a lofty opinion of economists, our financial media, the Federal Reserve or the European Central Bank (ECB). Am I frustrated with economists not doing their job? Yes. It reminds me of a story about President Truman.

Search for the One-Handed Economist

Harry Truman didn't have an economic background so he relied on his collection of Economic PhDs for advice. When he asked them about the impact of rising interest rates, he was looking for a straight answer. His Economists replied that ***on the one hand***, rising interest rates could slow economic growth, but, ***on the other hand***, rising interest rates could inhibit inflation. Truman was frustrated with his Economists. He said what he needed was a "One-Handed Economist". He needed a straight answer.

My frustration with economists is not the "one hand, other hand" problem of Truman but rather that the economists are not analyzing the problems we are facing correctly or completely. Economists seem to think that the world is entirely composed of interest rates, money supply and unemployment rates. They're not thinking "Outside the Box".

The Economist Box
Interest Rates Money Supply Inflation . .

Outside the Box

Derivatives
Leverage
Innovation
.
.

The world is simply more complex than just interest rates, money supply, inflation etc. For example, there are $600 Trillion of Derivatives that never are even mentioned by economists. This is a huge omission. Derivatives were a large part of the US 2008 Financial Panic and will be a large part of the coming Euro Meltdown.

Example: AIG Derivatives and the US 2008 Panic
The day after Lehman failed, AIG failed and was bailed out with $180 Bil of taxpayer money by the Federal Reserve. This was 100% due to AIG Derivatives [2-1]. By spending nearly 100% of their time worrying about interest rates, the Federal Reserve completely dropped the ball on analyzing the impact of Derivatives. The mission of the Federal Reserve is to prevent Financial Panics. They utterly failed because they failed to focus on one of the critical issues – Derivatives.

My Background
I am not an economist. What is my background? In a sentence, it is a combination of mathematics (BS), physics, engineering (MS), business (MBA) and being a pilot. With a

background like that, why am I writing a 2nd book on economics and finance?

The Reason Why I Write: The Wall St. Panic of 2008
In September 2008, Wall St. and the Federal Reserve panicked. Lehman failed followed the next day by AIG and one of the country's largest money market funds "broke the buck". It was utter chaos. The government responded by bailing out Fannie Mae ($180 Bil), Wall St. Banks (TARP = $750 Bil), AIG ($180 Bil) and topped it off with a Stimulus Bill ($800 Bil). ***That's a taxpayer cost of $1,910 Bil right there.*** But it got worse.   The stock market lost $5 Trillion and housing $3 Trillion. This was all attributed to the "Subprime Mess".

This was an absolutely inadequate explanation. Certainly there was an asset bubble in real estate, and there definitely was a large loss in Subprime Mortgages, but the size of the Subprime losses should never have caused $Trillions in damage.   I desperately wrote the Federal Reserve and every financial publication I knew showing that the Subprime losses were about $400 Bil (The FCIC estimate was $300 Bil [2-2]). It wasn't the end of the world. There was no reason for a Panic, Bailout or Stimulus!

Financial Crisis Inquiry Commission (FCIC)
As a result of the US Financial Crisis of 2008, a bipartisan commission was set up to analyze the causes, something the Federal Reserve should have done prior to the Crisis. I refer to this commission as the FCIC. In Appendix 1, I compare their conclusions to those of my book on the subject.

My Track Record: "The Wall St. Panic of 2008"

My book was written and published 6 months before the FCIC Report. In fact, I sent many members of that Commission a copy. First, I think my basic conclusions were the same of those of the FCIC. To me, this is confirmation of my ability to analyze. It is a plus for my track record. Second, did members of the FCIC actually read my book? I think so. They use an example of Synthetic Car Insurance which is very similar to my example of Synthetic Fire Insurance. It is not important that you understand what these examples are. It is just significant that they are very similar. No other book I have read on Derivatives even discusses the concept of "Insurable Interest." [2-3]

One Citizen vs. The Federal Reserve

The Federal Reserve has 21,000 people and flocks of Economic PhDs. If I assume the FCIC analysis of the Crisis is correct (and I do), then my analysis starting in September 2008 was better than that of the Federal Reserve or Treasury. Why? I am not afraid to _think_ and identify the important issues. In contrast, the Fed and most economists think the entire world can be explained by interest rates and money supply. They're trapped in an intellectual box of their own making. Try and find even a single document where an economist talks about the impact of Derivatives. I haven't been able to find one.

Why am I concerned about Derivatives? They are huge, invisible and have a tremendous impact on our financial system. The US GDP is $15 Tril but the Derivative market is a mind boggling **_$600 Tril_** [2-4]. Just a tiny $2 Tril sliver of this Derivative market ($2 Tril of Subprime Derivatives) played a huge role in bringing down our economy in 2008. Yet, the Fed doesn't even mention them. Is this incompetence or what?

The European Central Bank (ECB)

The ECB is the Fed for the Eurozone. Is it any more competent than our Fed? No. The ECB loudly proclaims that "Greece will not default". The ECB doesn't make the slightest remark about the $400 Tril of Interest Rate Swaps that could cripple their financial system. No, unfortunately the ECB is every bit as incompetent as our Federal Reserve.

When the ECB says, "Greece will not default", it is not giving European citizens the straight answer that President Truman was after. I don't know if this is because the ECB is trying to be politically correct or is simply incompetent. In saying that "Greece will default", I feel like the small Chinese boy who said, "The Emperor is wearing no clothes".

The Emperor is wearing no clothes

There are many versions of this story. Here is one. The Chinese Emperor was getting fitted for new gowns one day. Of course, no one ever contradicted or criticized the Emperor or they would lose their head. As the tailors were changing gown and the Emperor was naked for a moment, the Chief Advisor (and chief sycophant) walked in and praised the Emperor's new gown as the finest silk. The tailor was in a tough spot. If he contradicted the Chief Advisor, his head was going to roll so he chimed in and said that this was the best, most translucent silk available in the world. All the other underlings present chimed in saying the same. The Emperor was impressed and, since the day was very hot, decided to walk outside the Forbidden City in his new, translucent silk gown. Of course, the Chief Advisor sent on his minions to warn all the citizens to not say anything about the Emperor being naked or their heads would roll. It worked for everyone except one small boy who said, "The Emperor is wearing no clothes." Essentially, it took only one person to state the obvious.

In this book, I am going to state the obvious. The Greeks are going to default. Probably Ireland and Portugal will join them. With the default losses that Eurozone will suffer, the Euro will be in deep trouble. Derivatives will greatly amplify the damage. The existence of the Euro will be threatened.

"Economics is too important to be left to economists."
This Chapter explains briefly why I believe this is true. The economists of the Federal Reserve completely failed the American people in their primary duty to "prevent financial panics". The ECB is about to fail the people of the Eurozone by not taking the necessary steps to save the Euro. What are those steps? That is what this book is about.

Is this book an impartial 3rd person PhD thesis in Economics? Absolutely not. I will definitely give my analysis and my opinions on what is about to happen. Every last bit of data will not be carefully footnoted (I will cite some sources), but I will supply an extensive Bibliography of both books and websites. In certain cases (e.g, IMF data on Greece, Appendix 4), I will discuss data sources in detail. Is this book hubris or just an honest attempt at a warning before the Euro Crisis reaches the disintegration state? My aim is the latter, but you the reader can be the judge.

Chapter 3. Different Modes of Thinking

I'm not an economist so my approach to economics/finance will be different than that of most economists. I'm not going to argue about Keynesian or Supply Side economics. My approach will be different, and this Chapter will illustrate some of those differences. While I don't have a great deal of respect for the economists in the Fed or ECB, I do want to acknowledge that the subject of Economics is tough. The following story gives some idea of this.

Max Planck – Economic Dropout

As a part of our liberal education at Stanford, engineers and physicists had to take Econ 101. Our professor knew he was getting a crop of engineers/physicists who tended to look down their nose at the imprecise science of Economics. Consequently, he decided to get our attention with a story about Max Planck. Max was one of the Superstars of the world of Physics. He put the "quantum" in Quantum Mechanics. What we didn't know is that Max started his academic career in Economics and dropped out for something easier – Physics. Max was right. Economics is more difficult. In Physics, we isolate just one variable and test it. In Economics, there are hundreds of variable operating all the time and many of them are human. How can you develop any meaningful Economic Laws? It's nearly impossible. Physics is easier. Our professor concluded his little story by saying that if we needed to make some more giant leaps in Physics, he might be able to find another Econ dropout to help out.

There is absolutely no question that Economics and Finance is difficult. Does this mean we are helpless? Not all the time. As I will demonstrate in my Chapter on the Greek Death Spiral, simple math will supply the answer. However, the precise impact of \$400 Tril [3-1] of Derivatives subsequent to a Greek Default is nearly impossible to estimate accurately.

Despite the difficulty of the Economics/Finance subject matter, an effort must be made. The Euro Crisis is simply too important to ignore. Even if the best that can be done is a simple Ball Park analysis, this is better than nothing. Let me discuss how my Modes of Thinking differ from those of the average Economist.

Mode of Thinking I – Ball Park Thinking
I am going to make several predictions in this book. I am going to project that Greece will default, the European Bailout Fund will be inadequate and Derivatives will amplify the default losses. How can I possibly do this? Do I have enough information? Yes, I have enough information to do a Ball Park Analysis. That's enough analysis to come to the right conclusion even though the exact numbers might not be right. Let me illustrate what I mean with a story from my Quantum Mechanics Professor at Stanford.

How many barbers in the USA?
When my Professor went to his Oral Exam for his PhD in Physics, he wasn't quite ready for the first question he was asked:

How many barbers are there in the USA?

At first, he wondered if he was in the wrong room. Was this the committee for an Economic PhD? Then, after recovering from his initial shock, he realized that what they were really asking him was to _**think**_. What assumptions could he make? What deductions could he make? He started to speak. He said that he had his hair cut every month. It took the barber about 15 minutes to cut his hair (crew cut). His barber worked 40 hours/week, and he always had customers waiting for their turn. He did a little mental math and came up with a number of how many men his barber could cut hair for in a year. Then he estimated how many men there were in the USA. Dividing this number by his barber's production rate gave him an estimate for the number of barbers in the USA. Was his number precisely correct? Even the committee didn't know. What they were interested in was his "Ball Park Thinking".

I am going to predict that Greece will run through its 110 Billion Euro bailout in early 2012 and default on its debt at that time. Is this prediction precisely correct? It is probably not precisely correct, but I think it is in the Ball Park. Precision numbers are not a goal for this book. Good, fearless thinking is.

Ball Park Thinking is an important technique. However, even more important is the selection of the problem(s) that must be addressed whether we want to do so or not. The ECB and Brussels don't want to face the problem of a Greek Default and its ensuing fallout. They are in denial. This is a huge mistake on their part. In my terminology, what they lack is any type of Pilot Thinking.

Mode of Thinking II – Pilot Thinking

My definition of "Pilot Thinking" is that you must address the critical problems right away and not postpone analysis or "kick the can down the road". In my opinion, the ECB is simply "kicking the can down the road".

In addition to being an aircraft design and flight test engineer, I was a private pilot. There is a different type of thinking required if you are a pilot. You have to solve the problem that you are faced with not the problem you choose to solve. Furthermore, you have to solve the problem with the best information you have at the time. You don't have the luxury of waiting to acquire perfect and complete information. In fact, much critical data on the PIG default status is being kept deliberately secret. Despite this, an analysis should be done.

This Pilot Thinking is in complete contrast to the type of thinking of an academic economist. If the economist is not ready to put forward his solution to a particular problem, he can just put it off until next Monday. Try that with a failed engine. Or, if an economist doesn't like the problem he is working on, he can just choose another. Well, the failed engine problem chooses you.

What I am saying is that in analyzing the PIG crisis, it is necessary to address the important elements that contribute to it even if our knowledge of these elements is incomplete. For example, do we know the exact amount of bonds that Greece must refinance each year? Do we know what the Greek budget deficit will be for each of the next 3 years? No we don't, but we still must estimate what the likelihood of a Greek default will be. It is not as if we choose to solve the Greek default problem. It has essentially chosen us. Let me use a Pilot story to illustrate the necessity of solving the problem we are faced with.

Miracle on the Hudson

Probably everyone knows the story of the Miracle on the Hudson. A US Airways plane took off from LaGuardia and big Canadian geese were ingested into both engines which caused them to fail shortly thereafter. The pilot didn't choose to have a failed engines problem, but he had to solve it. With both engines gone, his plane acquired the aerodynamic characteristics of a rock. He knew he didn't have a lot of time to assess his data and make a decision. He knew he couldn't make it back to LaGuardia Airport (Plan A) or over to Teterboro Airport (Plan B) so he made a magnificent landing in the Hudson River (Plan C).

The type of thinking I am describing is familiar to every military leader. Any general would love to have perfect geographical knowledge, perfect weather knowledge and perfect knowledge about his enemy's location.

General Eisenhower and D-Day

Ike would love to have had perfect knowledge before D-Day. If he had known the Germans had recently moved a new division into the hills above Omaha Beach, he could have adjusted his plan to a different beach and avoided the horrendous losses there. Well, Ike didn't have perfect knowledge. He had to go with the best knowledge he had at

> the time. He had to plan and analyze with imperfect information. Then he had to decide whether the invasion was going to succeed or fail.

Are the economists of the ECB or the politicians of Brussels like Ike or the US Airway Pilot? I don't think so. I think they are taking the politically safe route of saying that Greece will not default. This way they can avoid any analysis or planning for the hard choices they should be making.

Mode of Thinking III – Chess Playing
I was a Chess player. In my days as an engineer, I would play Chess during our lunch time. In fact, at one time, I could even play with my back to the board. What is the key to winning in Chess? The key is that you have to think several moves ahead. The ECB isn't doing this. They are in denial about the coming Greek Default and not thinking about the next moves after the Default (see Chapter 17). If they persist in this, they will lose.

Scope of this book – "Magic + 1"
What I describe as Modes I, II and III of Thinking illustrate how my approach to the Euro Crisis will be different than that of most economists. In just the case of the Greek crisis, there is much more involved than simply deficits, debt and interest rates. There is the GDP growth or lack of growth, the political protests and much, much more. I will not attempt to take every factor into consideration. I can make the point that to help save the Euro, the following actions need to be taken: triage, pre-emption, protection from Derivatives and growth. I describe this as a "Magic +1" level analysis. Here is the story behind that term.

> **Magic, Magic +1 and Magic + 2**
> An aircraft engineer was on a remote Pacific Island talking to an aborigine when an airplane flew overhead. The aborigine asked the engineer to explain how it was possible for the plane to fly. The engineer wrote down the Lift Equation (Magic + 2). That was too complicated for the aborigine. He said, "I don't understand it." Then the engineer tried to explain it without equations by verbally describing the partial pressure on the upper surface of the wing (Magic + 1). No luck. The aborigine again said, "I don't understand it". Finally, in exasperation, the engineer simply said, "It's Magic." The aborigine smiled and said, "Ah Magic. That I understand."

The analysis presented in this book is at a simplified level. It is just one step above "Magic" (i.e., "Magic + 1"). Unfortunately, the more that the ECB and politicians proclaim that Greece will not default, the more they show that they are still stuck at the "Magic" level of thinking.

Finance is boring – like reading a Ketchup label
In her review of my book, my wife plowed through all the numbers and Tables. Her assessment was that this book is about as exciting as reading the label on a bottle of Ketchup. My wife's suggestion was to write this book as exciting as a romance novel or a mystery. Unfortunately, the subject of finance has all the romance of a Balance Sheet and excitement of an interest rate. The subject matter does not leave a lot to work with. While I realize that finance is boring, it is also vitally important to the economic well-being of our countries and everyone who is interested in getting a job or hanging on to

the one they have. A Euro Meltdown will adversely affect millions of people. To minimize the boring aspects of finance, I will try to fight back by making this book short and putting more detailed discussion in the Appendices and Notes

Addendum: Acronyms, Abbreviations and more

In the rear of the book is a list of Acronyms/Abbreviations that are used throughout this book. I have already used ECB, FCIC, Tril, Bil and more. If you forget what these mean, please refer to the Acronyms in the rear of the book.

I tend to capitalize words that I want to emphasize such as Derivatives. Teddy Roosevelt used to do this, and I picked up that bad habit from him.

Addendum: Condescending Manner

In addition to observing that this book reads like the label on a bottle of Ketchup, my wife also said that I write in a condescending manner. When I am commenting on the ECB, Fed, economists and financial media, this condescending manner is entirely intentional. When I am trying to make something clear to the reader, I am simply trying to be clear, not condescending.

Chapter 4. Basic Definitions

This Chapter is not going to be eloquent prose. It is just going to go over some basic definitions and concepts that will be used later in the book. While some might argue that this material belongs in an Appendix, I am afraid if I put it there, it would go unread. While reading the rest of the book, it may be useful to refer back to this chapter.

Dollars and Euros
Before even beginning with Basic Definitions, let me state that in this book all calculations are in Dollars with the following ratio: 1.3 Dollars to 1 Euro.

Part 4-1. Basic Definitions

What is a Financial Death Spiral?

Definition: Financial Death Spiral
It begins with a country that has a large National Debt and a large yearly governmental budget deficit. Each year the deficit adds to the National Debt making it larger and larger. The country has to borrow new money from the bond market in order to finance its ever increasing debt, and the bond market demands a higher and higher interest rate each year. Finally, the country can either pay the interest no more or cannot obtain financing from the bond market. The country defaults at the end of its Financial Death Spiral. Lucky countries get bailed out instead of defaulting. However, the bailouts may just

> postpone a default if the painful steps of financial reform are not taken.

The Greeks already had one Death Spiral. In the middle of 2010, their National Debt and Budget Deficits were so high that the Mean Bond Market demanded 20% interest on the new Greeks bonds that they were attempting to sell. This was an unsustainable interest rate. However, instead of ending in default, the Greeks managed to persuade the Eurozone for a bailout. Iceland went through its Financial Death Spiral in 2008 without a bailout. It defaulted on everything and suffered a huge devaluation of its currency as well as being excluded from borrowing from the world bond market. It dropped from be the Viking banking raiders back to fishing, making aluminum and stuff it knows. It returned to reality.

Let me make some other basic definitions:

Definition: Gross Domestic Product (GDP)
This is what a country creates in economic value each year. It is analogous to what salary a person earns each year. The GDP of the US is $15 Trillion for 2010. The Eurozone GDP is $12 Trillion.

Definition: National Debt
This is essentially what a country has borrowed from when it first became a country up until the present. The National Debt of the US is about $14.3 Trillion which is nearly 100% of our $15 Trillion GDP.

Definition: Budget Deficit
The yearly budget deficit is simply the government expenditures for the year minus the taxes received by the government for the year. For 2010, it was 14% of GDP for Greece and 10% GDP for the US.

As a result of the Wall St. Panic of 2008, the Treasury/Fed pleaded for a bank rescue fund which was called TARP. This totaled $750 Bil in funds. The Eurozone has constructed a similar fund. It is a little more complicated (everything in Europe always is more complicated). The Europeans were clever enough to get the International Monetary Fund, IMF, involved so the rest of the world contributes roughly 1/3 of the funds. Even though this fund is mostly Eurozone and partly world I am going to define it in this book as the EuroTARP fund.

Definition: EuroTARP
The combined fund from Eurozone and IMF sources which has been formed to bail out Eurozone countries and which will probably be used to bail out Eurozone banks when Defaults occur. It is $1,000 Bil or $1 Trillion.

Which countries in the Eurozone are liable to suffer a Financial Death Spiral? This Magic + 1 level book is just going to consider three – Greece, Ireland and Portugal.

Definition: PIG Countries
This refers to Portugal, Ireland and Greece.

23

Additionally, two other countries are considered in danger – Spain and Italy. Consequently, you will see another term in the financial media.

Definition: PIIGS Countries
This is simply the PIG countries + Spain and Italy.

Definition: Re-structuring of Debt
Re-structuring is a nice word for default. Since many people do not understand re-structuring, it is used to confuse them.

Part 4-2. Bond Definitions

Bonds are absolutely critical to understanding why Greece will default. The following is a Magic + 1 definition of basic bond concepts. Bonds are actually more complicated than explained below, but the following definitions are good enough for a Ball Park analysis.

Definition: Government Bond
A government bond is a loan from one party (e.g., a bank or taxpayer) to the government. The lending party gives the government a sum (e.g., $1,000) for a fixed period of time (e.g., 1 year) at a fixed interest rate (e.g., 3%). The lending party will receive $30 in interest payments and then receive its principal (e.g., $1,000) back at the end of the bond period or maturity (e.g., 1 year). When the bond is initially issued it is called the primary bond market. When it is later traded, it is called the secondary bond market.

Definition: Default
If a country cannot pay either the interest payment due or pay back the bond principal, it is said to have defaulted. In 2002, Argentina defaulted on $120 Billion of its National Debt. Did this mean that its bondholders lost all $120 Billion? No. They lost $100 Billion. Argentina did pay $20 Billion or roughly 20 cents on the dollar.

Definition: Bond Rollover
Let's say a country has $100 Billion in bonds. Of these, $10 Billion have a 1 year maturity (i.e., they must be paid back at the end of 1 year), $10 Billion with a 2 year maturity and $10 Billion due at end years 3 thru 10. Then each year, the country must either have enough excess cash to pay the $10 Billion entirely or it must go to the bond market and borrow a new bond of $10 Billion to pay the old bond off. This refinancing of bonds each year is called bond rollover or bond redemption or bond refinance.

Generally Greek bonds have a 10 year maturity. A good first approximation of how many bonds will have to be rolled over each year is to take National Debt/10. Since the Greek National Debt is $430 Bil, the anticipated bond rollover each year is $430/10 = $43 Bil.

Definition: Mean Bond Market
This refers to the worldwide group of banks or investors that are interested in buying a country's bonds. Will this group of investors be willing to buy every country's bonds at the same

interest rate? No. A German Bond is much more reliable than a Portuguese Bond. Consequently, the investors will buy a German bond paying 3% interest while they will demand 10% from the Portuguese. The interest rate depends upon the risk that the investors see in a country's bond. Can any country in bad financial shape expect sympathy from the bond market? No. It is a Mean Bond Market. The Mean Bond Market is currently demanding 28% (June 2011) on Greek Bonds in the Secondary Market. That's mean. Please see Appendix 2 for an explanation of the Secondary Market.

Secondary Bond Market

When a bond is first issued, it is called the primary bond market. Some bond holders may not want to hold the bond to maturity so they trade it. When they trade it, this is called the secondary bond market. It is kind of like buying a selling a house. When a new house is built, it would be sold in the primary market. When it is resold for a higher or lower price, it is sold in the secondary market. See Appendix 2 for further discussion.

$600 Trillion of Derivatives

I will refer over and over again to the $600 Trillion of Derivatives and $400 Trillion of Interest Rate Swaps. This is documented at the Bank of International Settlements website: www.bis.org; go to the Statistics tab, then choose: Semiannual OTC Derivative Statistics at end-Dec 2010; then download number 19: Amount of over-the-counter (OTC) derivatives by risk category and instrument (PDF). Or try: http://www.bis.org/statistics/otcder/dt1920a.pdf

Part 2. Financial Death Spiral

Chapter 5. Financial Death Spiral

What is a Financial Death Spiral? At a Magic + 1 level, the Financial Death Spiral has three basic elements:

1. A National Debt at or above 100% GDP
2. A yearly budget deficit near 10% GDP
3. Bond Rollover or Bond Re-financing

In order to start out as simply as possible, the Financial Death Spiral for Country PIG will be illustrated with just two of the above elements: (1) National Debt and (2) Budget Deficits. In Chapter 6, I will also include (3) Bond Rollover for the Greek Death Spiral.

To illustrate the Death Spiral, we first must make some assumptions about a hypothetical country named PIG.

Table 5-1. Assumptions about Country PIG
GDP = $100 Bil National Debt = 100% of GDP = $100 Bil Yearly Budget Deficit = 10% GDP = $10 Bil

Can I illustrate the Death Spiral for Country PIG without Tables or calculations? Unfortunately, I can't. What is the Death Zone for a country's National Debt? Generally a National Debt that is 160% GDP is considered unsustainable.

For Country PIG with a National Debt of $100 Bil, the Death Zone for National Debt is 160% GDP or $160 Bil.

Table 5-2 simply illustrates the effect of Budget Deficits that remain uncorrected. If the Budget Deficit for each year is $10 Bil, it will simply increase the National Debt by $10 Bil each year.

Table 5-2. PIG Death Spiral (Budget Deficit only)		
.	(1)	(2)	
Year	Beginning Nat Debt	Budget Deficit	Ending Nat Debt
2010	100	10	110
2011	110	10	120
2012	120	10	130
2013	130	10	140
2014	140	10	150
2015	150	10	**160**Death Zone

The Table above is read from left to right. For year 2010, the Beginning National Debt is $100 Bil. The Budget Deficit is $10 Bil. These two columns are added together to determine the last column, the Ending National Debt of $110 Bil. The Ending National Debt of 2010 becomes the Beginning National Debt of 2011, and the process begins again.

What Table 5-2 shows is that the yearly Budget Deficit of $10 Bil has nowhere to go except to add on to the existing National Debt. Table 5-2 shows that in 6 short years, country PIG has reached a National Debt = 160 Bil or 160% GDP.

Some might argue that defining the Death Zone as 160% GDP is not correct. They could point to Japan which has a National Debt = 200% GDP. Japan is an exception as I will explain below.

The Exception of Japan

The National Debt of Japan is 200% of its GDP. Why hasn't it defaulted? There are two reasons:

(1) The Japanese have ***always paid 1% interest*** or less on their bonds. Thus, even though its National Debt is $10 Trillion, its interest payments are a relatively low $100 Bil/year. With a GDP of $5 Trillion, this is manageable. Who is willing to buy Japanese bonds that only pay 1% per year interest? Answer: the Japanese.

(2) The second reason that the Japanese can survive with 200% GDP of National Debt is that the Japanese banks and ***Japanese citizens loyally buy Japanese national bonds***. They could get higher interest if they bought German bonds at 3% or Portuguese bonds at 10%, but the Japanese are very, very loyal. They buy Japanese bonds.

Greeks don't buy Greek bonds (except for small amounts). Therefore Greece is dependent upon the Mean Bond Market.

Lesson for the US

The US National Debt is about 100% GDP. That means we are at the starting place of Country PIG. Our Budget Deficits for the past 2 years and for years projected forward are 10% GDP. This is exactly the assumption made for Country PIG. What this suggests is that if our budget deficits remain unchanged,

> we could be in a Financial Death Spiral just like Greece. The Lesson for the US is to watch Greece closely. When the impact of the Greece default is apparent, the US should observe this painful lesson and avoid a similar Greek Tragedy.

Advanced Financial Death Spiral in Appendix 3

My wife says that reading all these Death Spiral Tables is about as exciting as reading the label on a bottle of Ketchup. I can't dispute that. Finance is boring. But it is also vitally important. This Chapter dealt with just 2 Death Spiral elements:

1. A National Debt at or above 100% GDP
2. A yearly budget deficit near 10% GDP

The next Chapter will include the 3rd element, bond rollover, for the Greek Death Spiral:

1. A National Debt at or above 100% GDP
2. A yearly budget deficit near 10% GDP
3. Bond Rollover

I am going to show how the additional requirement of Bond Rollover will help Greece run through its 3 year Bailout Funds in less than 2 years. What I am not going to show is that the situation is really worse. As a country's National Debt grows, the Mean Bond Market which is supplying the money for the additional Budget Deficits and Bond Rollovers will demand higher and higher interest rates. I will not burden the reader with more numbers here, but, for the more courageous, I recommend that you read Appendix 3. I show how a 10% or 20% interest rate (what the Mean Bond Market was demanding from Greece in 2010) will move the National Debt Death Zone forward in time from 2015 (shown in Table 5-2) to 2012 (20% interest).

Chapter 6. Greek Death Spiral

31

Warning: This Chapter contains Tables
If you are tired of reading Tables, you can just trust me that Greece will default in early 2012 and proceed to the next Chapter. If you need a little more convincing that Greece will default, then you must plow through the Tables of this Chapter and even compare my estimates to those of the International Monetary Fund (IMF) which I do in Appendix 4.

6-1. Simple Death Spiral
In this Chapter I will expand the Death Spiral of Chapter 5 by adding element (3), Bond Rollover. First, let me compare the assumptions made for Country PIG with the real world situation of Greece.

Table 6-1. Comparison of Country PIG with Greece (Numbers in $ Billions)		
	PIG	Greece
GDP	$100	$330
National Debt (% GDP)	100%	130%
National Debt ($)	$100	$430
Budget Deficit	10% GDP	10% GDP
Budget Deficit ($)	$10	$33

Right off the bat, it can be seen that Greece is starting from a worse position than Country PIG. First, its National Debt is already at the 130% level.   Remember, it took only 6 short years for PIG to reach the end of its Death Spiral. It will take Greece less time.   For comparison, I will show the Death Spirals for Country PIG and Greece below:

Table 5-2. PIG Death Spiral (Budget Deficit only)			
.	(1)	(2)	
Year	Beginning Nat Debt	Budget Deficit	Ending Nat Debt
2010	100	10	110
2011	110	10	120
2012	120	10	130
2013	130	10	140
2014	140	10	150
2015	150	10	**160**Death Zone

Table 6-2. Greek Death Spiral – Budget Deficit = 10%GDP			
Year	Begin Nat Debt	Budget Deficit	End Nat Debt
2011	430	33 (10% GDP)	463
2012	463	33	496
2013	480	33	529 (160% GDP)Death Zone

A comparison of Tables 5-2 and 6-2 shows that if Greece maintains a 10% GDP Budget Deficit, it will beat Country PIG to the Death Zone for National Debt (3 years vs. 6 years).

Greece already reached its Death Zone at only 130% GDP in the middle of 2010 when the Mean Bond Market refused to buy its bonds except at a 20% interest rate. Greece was saved from the Death Zone by the Eurozone Bailout of $143 Bil which was supposed to last for 3 years. This bailout was supposed to finance both its Budget Deficits and Bond Rollovers. Will it?

6-2 How long will the Greek bailout funds last?

> ### Critical Question
> Will the Greek bailout of $143 Billion last for 3 years?

As the following Table shows, Greece is going to suffer a second Death before the end of the 3 year period. It will default in early 2012 when it runs out of Bailout Funds.

Table 6-3. How long does the Bailout Fund last for Greece? [6-1]

Year	Begin Bailout	Rollover Required	Budget Deficit	End Bailout
½ 2010	143	-21	-23	99
2011	99	-43	-33	23
2012	23	-43	-33	-53 (**Default**)
½ 2013	-53	-21	-17	-91

This Table has a different format and is slightly more complicated than the Tables I have shown previously. I give a more detailed description of the Table on the following pages.
Table 6-3 shows (white row) that Greece will run through its 3 year bailout fund in less than 2 years. It will run out of funds in early 2012. At that time, it can turn to the Mean Bond Market to sell its bonds, but the Mean Bond Market is demanding 20% interest rates (see Appendix 3 for further discussion). A 20% interest rate is unsustainable, and Greece will default.

> ## Table 6-3 is the most important Table of this book
> This Table is my statement that Greece will default in early 2012. This is in direct opposition to the repeated statements from the ECB that Greece will not default. In 2012, we will see who has more credibility.

Trust me or check me [6-2]

If the Tables and numbers are overwhelming you at this point, you can simply trust me that I am right in saying Greece will default in early 2012. The white highlighted rows of each Table tells the story.

For those that are a little more skeptical, let me suggest that you check my data with that of the International Monetary Fund (IMF) which I do in Appendix 4. Also, let me explain Table 6-3 in detail (for those readers who love numbers).

Detailed Explanation for Table 6-3

Since Table 6-3 is so important, let me describe it in a clear (not condescending) manner. First, I have ½ 2010 and ½ 2013. This is because the bailout started in the middle of 2010 and was to last 3 years until the middle of 2013. Second, instead of the familiar "Beginning Nat Debt" in the 1st column, I have "Begin Bailout". This is because the critical parameter is the Bailout and not the National Debt. If Greece runs out of Bailout Funds, it will default. It doesn't have to reach 160% GDP.

The 2nd column is labeled "Rollover Required". This refers to the Bond Rollover required by Greece for each year. Greece has $430 Bil in National Debt. This is roughly turned over in a

10 year period. Therefore $430/10 = $43 Bil of bonds that must be re-financed each year. In other words, in 2001, Greece issued $43 Bil of 10 year bonds. Since some of these bonds mature in 2011, they must either be paid off (Greece can't do that) or Greece must re-finance them (which it can do with Bailout funds). Since ½ 2010 is a half year, I assume $21 Bil must be re-financed that year (i.e., 21 is roughly half of 43).

The 3rd column is the Budget Deficit. I assume a steady 10% GDP for the Budget Deficit each year. Greece has promised to institute reforms to bring this deficit down, but street protests have prevented this from happening. The Budget Deficit for ½ 2010 has occurred. The Budget Deficit for 2010 was 14% GDP so I have shown 7% GDP or $21 Bil. We are nearly half way through 2011 and every indication is that the Budget Deficit will be in the neighborhood of 10% GDP. Even if Greece managed to zero out its deficit for 2012, it would be too late to avoid a default.

The 4th column is the Ending amount of the Bailout funds for the year. In 2012, this is -53 Bil. This means that Greece ran out of Bailout Funds during 2012 and $53 Bil in the hole. At this point, Greece will default.

Math Challenge for the ECB
The 3 year Bailout Funds for Greece total $143 Bil. Can the ECB simply add up the bond rollover amounts required for these 3 years as well as the actual/estimated budget deficits for these 3 years and show me how they total up to less than $143 Bil? Can the ECB show where my Table 6-3 is wrong?

I'm sending a copy of this book to the ECB, but I'm not going to hold my breath for their response. I think they will continue the politically correct denial that Greece will default.

Addendum: Saving Greece

> **Saving Greece**
> As I end this analysis, I would like to say that I fervently do not want the Greeks to default. Greece is the cradle of Western Civilization. It brought us Socrates, Plato, Aristotle, Euclid, Pythagoras, Archimedes and so much more. I have traveled to Greece several times and enjoy both the old classic ruins as well as the friendly Greek people. The people of Iceland are also wonderful. Unfortunately, this didn't save them from default. All the facts on Greece point towards default. I think there is a very slim chance to avoid such a disaster. I have written a plan (See Appendix 5) that I think could save the Greeks from default. Unfortunately, I do not see them showing the necessary unity nor taking the necessary steps at present. They have only 1 year to take decisive action.

Chapter 7. Impact of PIG Defaults

The impact of PIG Defaults is a vast subject. The full impact will include not only the Defaults but also the amplification of this damage by Derivatives. However, the impact of Derivatives will be addressed in Part 3 of this book. This chapter will merely focus on in three areas: 7-1 EuroTARP, 7-2 Eurozone Bank Capital and 7-3 Eurozone Growth.

7-1. Impact on the EuroTARP fund

The EuroTARP fund originally had $1,000 Brillion committed to it. At present approximately $343 Billion has been committed to the PIG bailouts. How does *the remaining $657 Billion* compare to estimated PIG Defaults?

My prediction is that Greece will default on its National Debt in early 2012. I believe this will precipitate similar Defaults by Ireland and Portugal also within 2012. Once confidence is lost, the situation will get ugly in a hurry. In the Table below, I show the size of Defaults if 100% of the National Debt was defaulted on as well as my likely prediction.

Table 7-1. Default Size Estimates [7-1]		
Country	100% Default	Likely Default
Greece	$500 Bil	$300 Bil
Ireland	$200 Bil	$100 Bil
Portugal	$200 Bil	$100 Bil
Total	$900 Bil	$500 Bil

Comparing the size of either assumption for Defaults, it appears that the remaining EuroTARP funds of $657 Bil are large enough to compensate for the damage at my low end estimate of $500 Billion, but insufficient at the high end estimate of $900 Billion Unfortunately, I think the problem will rapidly enlarge due to contagion and Derivatives.

Definition: Contagion
This is a relatively new term in the world of finance. Basically it means that if there is a loss of confidence in one area, it will spread to other areas.

An example of contagion is that if Portugal fails, the Spanish may also fail because they hold a large amount of Portuguese debt.

Table 7-2. Impact of PIG Defaults on EuroTARP

PIG Default range	$500-$900 Billion
EuroTARP remaining	$657 Billion

Ireland
Most of the PIIGS suffer from Welfare State abuse. They promise more than they can pay for and run up Budget Deficits and National Debt. Ireland's problem is different. It is like Iceland. It allowed its banking sector to run out of control. The banking sector lent to the Irish real estate sector which was Tulip Mania 2.

> **The Dutch Tulip Mania of the 1600s**
> Dutch tulips are varied and beautiful. In the prosperous 1600s, some Dutch started paying more and more for prized tulip varieties. As the prices went up, more Dutch got involved paying increasing higher prices – the herd instinct. Finally, the price of one bulb was the price of a house. Someone decided that a house was worth more than a tulip bulb and the whole asset bubble deflated.

A few years ago, my wife and I toured Ireland and stayed at a nice B&B near Shannon. I asked the woman what the price of her house was. My gosh. It was the price of a house in Southern California except in Ireland it rains every day of the year. Anecdotally, this was an indication of wildly overpriced real estate (and, of course, Southern California had its own real estate asset bubble).

Ireland got in trouble with its out of control banks, but the real disaster was in 2008 when the government ***guaranteed*** the bank loans. In Iceland, the government ***did not guarantee*** the loans of its banks. The result was that all the banks went bust along with the stock market, and the currency was devalued by 50%. By guaranteeing its banks' loans, the Irish government avoided an immediate default like Iceland, but it has just postponed the inevitable. Ireland has about a $200 Bil GDP but a staggering $870 Bil [7-2] in bank debt. Furthermore, the value of the real estate that serves as collateral for these loans are wildly overvalued. Ireland's coming default could be as bad as Greece's, but I make a more modest estimate in Table 7-1.

Nature of EuroTARP

Is there a pot of money totaling $1,000 Bil sitting in the bank vaults of the ECB in Frankfurt, Germany? No. EuroTARP is a pledge by the 17 countries of the Eurozone to come up with the money to protect their Euro. Some of these countries are in a weak position such as Spain, Italy and Belgium. If they need to ante up money for EuroTARP, it correspondingly weakens their own position. This makes it more likely that EuroTARP may have to come to their aid (e.g., Belgium, Spain etc.).

7-2. Impact of PIG Defaults on Eurozone Bank Capital

I am not going to go through a thorough estimation of the capital of Eurozone banks. In my Ball Park Analysis approach, I will simply estimate that it is less than the capital of the major Wall St. Banks in 2008. In my previous book, I estimated the bank capital for these banks at $800 Bil (see Appendix 8. Bank Capital and Subprime Losses in "The Wall St. Panic of 2008").

If the bank capital for Eurozone banks totals $800 Bil, then this amount can be compared to the estimated Default losses shown in Table 7-1 above. If the Default loss range is $500-$900 Bil, it is easy to see that these would wipe out most Eurozone banks. The fact that the EuroTARP fund was created is obviously a wise step in the right direction.

Table 7-3. PIG Defaults and Eurozone Bank Capital	
Estimate of Eurozone Bank Capital	$800 Bil
PIG Defaults	$500-900 Bil

7-3. Impact of PIG Defaults on Eurozone Growth

One of the critical issues that receives absolutely no coverage in the financial media is the impact of the PIG bailouts and potential PIG defaults on Eurozone Growth. The Eurozone suffers from a low economic growth rate of about 1% GDP per year.

Table 7-4. Eurozone Growth vs. Bailouts, Defaults	
Eurozone GDP (2010)	$12 Trillion [7-3]
5 years growth at 1% GDP	$600 Bil
Estimated PIG Defaults	$500-900 Bil

The ugly observation to be made from Table 7-4 is that a low estimate of PIG Defaults ($500 Bil) will eat up nearly 5 years of Eurozone growth. At the high end ($900 Bil), it will eat up nearly a decade of growth. PIG Defaults alone could cause a decade of Eurozone stagnation and, in Part 3, I will show that it will likely be even worse.

The Eurozone growth in good years is about 1% GDP. Germany is doing best with a robust (for Europe) growth of 2% GDP. Europe's growth problem is that it suffers from Eurosclerosis (from Multiple Sclerosis).

Definition: Eurosclerosis
The Europeans have chosen the Welfare State with its state health care, generous unemployment benefits and generous (and early) retirement benefits over a robust, growth oriented

> economy. They would prefer to have 2 hour lunches and 6 weeks of vacation/year vs. an economy that grew at 5% GDP. They reject the American Rat Race of only 2 weeks of vacation/year.

The attractions of a Welfare State are obvious. You don't really have to worry about a job, healthcare or retirement. All of this comes to you from the State (i.e., taxpayers).

The downside of the Welfare State has been demonstrated by the fall of the Soviet Union. It was the ultimate cradle to grave Welfare State. However, when the Soviet Union fell, it was pretty obvious that this was not an economic model for economic progress. The contrast between East and West Germany is a very good illustration of this. It has taken the West 20 years of subsidized support to try and bring the East up to Western prosperity, and the task is far from complete.

The Welfare States of the Eurozone are not nearly as bad as the Soviet Union and its eastern satellite countries. Approximately half the Welfare State economies are private so there is some economic dynamism. The private half of the economy supplies the government half. However, the Eurozone has been content with economic growth of only 1% GDP and therefore economic mediocrity. It has consciously chosen "less work" over "more growth".

The result of this Faustian bargain is that when the Eurozone desperately needs "growth" to solve its problems, it doesn't have any. Take a long look at Table 7-4. Just the 3 bailouts ($343 Bil) to the PIG countries have taken an enormous bite out of the Eurozone's anemic growth (1% GDP) for the next 5 years. If the Eurozone must absorb Defaults in the range of $500-900 Bil, it may mean essentially no economic growth for 10 years. If Spain were added to the Default list, the Eurozone would be going economically backwards.

Comparison of Subprime Losses to Default Losses
To get some idea of the size of the PIG Default losses, it is useful to compare them to the Subprime Losses that triggered the Wall St. Panic of 2008. My estimate for the Subprime Losses was $400 Bil and the estimate from the FCIC Report was in the same neighborhood [2-2]. Thus, the Subprime Losses are exceeded by the PIG Default estimates of $500-900 Bil. The Eurozone is probably in a weaker position than the US was in 2008 which means similar or worse economic carnage is possible. The creation of the US TARP program of $750 Bil made it possible to potentially double the capital of US banks. Similarly, EuroTARP can help Eurozone banks if the aid is handled properly.

Table 7-5 Comparison of PIG Defaults and Subprimes	
Subprime Failures	$400 Bil
PIG Defaults	$500-900 Bil
US TARP and Stimulus	$1,550 Bil
EuroTARP left	$ 657 Bil

The Eurozone is in a potentially more dangerous position than the US was in 2008, and the US did not handle the situation too well (see: "The Wall St. Panic of 2008"). The US Fed had a lot more money to throw at the problem than the ECB does.

Chapter 8. Triage and Preparation

Triage

When a military doctor faces three badly wounded soldiers and cannot treat them all, he must choose the best course of action and treat the most likely to survive. This is an example of triage. The ECB is not faced with three badly wounded soldiers. It is faced with a choice between helping three PIG countries in a Financial Death Spiral or preserving the Euro for the remaining 14 countries in the Eurozone. It must choose to preserve the Euro. The message of this book is:

Message of this book
It is far, far more important to preserve the Euro than it is to continually try and keep the PIG countries on the Euro with continual bailouts. It is far, far more important to help the European banks adversely affected by PIG Defaults than it is to help the PIG countries.

When Greece runs out of Bailout Funds in early 2012, they will ask the Eurozone for a 2nd bailout (in fact, they are asking in June 2011). The answer must be an emphatic "NO". The ECB was more than generous to help Greece with the 1st bailout. It cannot do more for Greece. Greece will be banished to an Icelandic Hell. It will not be any more pleasant for the Greeks than it is for the Icelanders. However, the ECB must concentrate on saving the Euro.

A 2nd Greek Bailout?

When I began writing this book in January 2011, there was no discussion of a Greek Default. At least there is discussion now. However, the discussion is headed in the wrong direction. Instead of emphasizing a "controlled Greek Default", the economists and politicians of the Eurozone are crafting a 2nd Greek bailout of approximately $160 Billion (the exact amount is under discussion). First, this 2nd Greek Bailout will continue to drain the EuroTARP fund. Second, it will send exactly the wrong message to Ireland and Portugal (i.e., you don't really have to zero out your deficit because you can get a 2nd Bailout too).

Let me make an estimate of the total of these PIG bailouts.

Table 8-1 PIG Bailouts	
1st Greek Bailout	$143 Bil
2nd Greek Bailout	$160 Bil
Irish Bailout	$100 Bil
Portuguese Bailout	$100 Bil
Total Bailouts	$503 Bil

Now let me use my low and high estimate for Default losses combined with this new Bailout total. Let me compare these new totals to the EuroTARP fund. Let me also compare these totals to 5 years of Eurozone economic growth.

Table 8-2 Bailouts + Defaults ($ Billions)		
Item	Low	High
Defaults	500	900
Bailouts	503	503
Total	1,003	1,403
Compared to:		
EuroTARP	1,000	1,000
5 yr Eurozone Growth	600	600

It is true that some fraction [8-1] of the Bailout money will be included in the Defaults. Nevertheless, the final amount of money is getting very close to the total EuroTARP funds. As I will show in Part 3, Defaults will not be the only losses. If we compare the Bailout total (including a 2nd Greek Bailout) to 5 years of Eurozone growth, it nearly consumes all of it. 2nd Bailouts to Ireland and Portugal would easily raise the total to an amount greater than 5 years of Eurozone growth. Can anyone spell ECONOMIC STAGNATION?

Bailout the Banks and not the PIGs
The more the ECB bails out the PIG countries, the larger their National Debts will become and the more painful will be the eventual Defaults. The ECB should take smaller losses sooner than larger losses later. The more the ECB spends of future Eurozone Growth, the more likely it is that the Eurozone will enter a prolonged period of Economic Stagnation or even

Depression. The ECB should not be helping the PIGs. It should be helping the Eurozone banks that will be harmed by PIG Defaults. These Defaults will not be the only problem facing the Eurozone as I will illustrate in Part 3. Derivatives.

Note on "Banks"

When I am referring to European Banks [8-2], I mean all European financial institutions which could mean regional governments, ECB etc. I'm trying to keep this book simple so I just say banks.

Let me return to the question of helping the PIGS and triage. If a Doctor is faced with 4 patients and 3 patients are dying, and he only has enough plasma to do a good job on one patient, shouldn't he use the EuroTARP plasma for the patient that is going to live? (Let's hope the Euro lives.)

Part 3. Derivatives

Chapter 9. What are Derivatives?

What are Derivatives and why will they make the Euro Crisis worse? These are complicated questions, and it will take me a few Chapters to even give a cursory answer to those questions.

Is the subject matter important? It is vitally important. The losses from Derivatives may easily exceed the losses due to PIG Defaults. If the ECB is not aware of Derivatives, it could very well get blindsided by something entirely unexpected and watch the Euro Crisis turn into a Euro Depression. At this point let me just observe that the GDP for the entire Eurozone was approximately $12 Trillion for the year 2010. By contrast the Derivative market is $600 Trillion or approximately 50 times larger than the Eurozone GDP. Just a 1% change in value in the $600 Trillion Derivative market is a mind boggling $6 Trillion which will dwarf the worst case 100% Default by Greece of $500 Billion or $0.5 Trillion.

Warning on Derivatives
The $600 Trillion [2-4] Derivative market is so huge that it dwarfs all banks and the GDPs of the US and Eurozone. Something so huge must be understood as best possible.

If the Derivative market is so huge and potentially influential on our economic system, why is no one writing about it? The principal reason is because the Derivative market is ***secret***. As a general rule, most Derivatives do not trade on a public exchange where their trades could be seen by the Public. They trade in Dark Pools that are unseen. Furthermore, Derivatives are carefully kept off Balance Sheets or buried in the footnotes to these financial statements. If you can't see Derivatives, it is tough to write about them. Nevertheless, I will fearlessly make an attempt.

What are Derivatives?

What are Derivatives? Few Americans and even fewer Europeans know. In 2008, I was on a tour of Greece with 25 other Americans. It was a very interesting and varied group of people. One was even from the SEC (our stock market regulator). In fact, he was one of the top 6 managers there. I eagerly asked me to explain to me what a Derivative was. He couldn't. This certainly says a lot about the SEC, but it is also an indication of the almost complete ignorance of what Derivatives are by the general public.

Simplified Definition of Derivatives
It is a contract based on an asset, index or condition.

This definition probably doesn't help too much. Let me proceed with some necessary concepts and examples.

Key Concept – Risk Transfer

One of the original purposes of Derivative contracts was to "transfer risk". Let me give an example of "risk transfer" with the example of Fire Insurance for a house.

Example: Fire Insurance and Risk Transfer
I own a house worth $400,000. If it burns down, I have nothing. That is a risk to me. I want to protect myself against losing my house in a fire. Therefore I buy Fire Insurance from an Insurance Company. I pay the Insurance Company a premium of $500 a year and, in return, the Insurance Company will pay me $400,000 if my house burns down. There is a contract between me and a Counter Party (the Insurance Company). I have "transferred risk" to the Insurance Company.

Definition: Counter Party
In a Derivative contract, there are two parties. The bank/company on one end of the contract, and the bank/company on the other end of the contract, the Counter Party. In the above example, I am the originating party, and the Insurance Company is my Counter Party. The term Counter Party is used in all Derivative Contracts.

The idea of "risk transfer" is a key concept behind Derivative contracts. Let me give some examples:

Example. Futures Contract on Oil Prices
If I am an airline, I can hedge against the price of oil going up by buying a Futures Contract on the price of oil. Let's say my airline will be profitable if the price of oil stays below $100 per barrel for the next year. If it goes above $100, I will lose money. Therefore I can hedge against the price of oil going above $100 per barrel by buying an Oil Futures Contract which guarantees me 10,000 barrels of oil at $100 per barrel for a

> period of 1 year. This Futures Contract is a Derivative based on a condition (i.e., the price of oil going above $100 per barrel).

This Oil Futures Contract is an example of a Derivative that is based on a condition (the price of oil rising above a certain level). Futures contracts have been around for 150 years, and they work. The Commodities Futures Trading Commission (CFTC) regulates them which **_enhances_** rather than inhibits their trading. All Futures Contracts are traded on public exchanges so everyone in the Public can know their price. The CFTC also regulates that Futures Contracts are settled daily.

Example: Daily Settlement

In the above Futures Contract, let's assume that the price of oil goes to $102 per barrel. The Counter Party to the airline in this contract must then put $2 per barrel in an escrow account. If oil goes up to $110 the next day, the Counter Party must put in another $8 per barrel. At the end of the Futures Contract period of 1 year, the airline will get the difference between the actual oil price (say $120 per barrel) and $100. The CFTC makes sure that a Futures Contract is a real promise with money in the bank (or escrow account) vs. an empty promise.

Let me give another example of a Derivative contract that is similar to insurance – Credit Default Swaps.

Example: Credit Default Swap

Let's say I own a $1 Billion bond from Bank A. I have a risk that Bank A will go bankrupt, and I may lose all my money invested in the bond. Therefore, I want to get insurance against losing this money. I can do so by buying a Credit Default Swap. I transfer my risk of bond failure to a Counter Party that is willing to pay me the full $1 Billion for the bond in return for me paying a small premium to the Counter Party. The Counter Party could be a bank or hedge fund or any other willing party.

If I substitute the bond for my house in the earlier example, a Credit Default Swap is acting just like insurance. One might wonder why it isn't called Credit Default Insurance. It isn't called insurance because then it would be regulated by a State Insurance Commissioner. Credit Default Swaps are totally unregulated by either States or the Federal government, and the Derivative makers want to keep it that way.

Let me give an example of a Derivative based on an asset -- Subprime Mortgages. This, of course, was the type of Derivative that was most dangerous during the Wall St. Panic of 2008.

Example: Subprime Mortgage Derivative
Let's say I am a Wall St. bank and own 1,000 Subprime Mortgages. I want to transfer the risk of these mortgages failing to customers. I do this by dividing up the pool of mortgages into 10 Derivative layers or tranches. Each layer contains roughly 100 mortgages. While the bank still holds the mortgages, the risk has been transferred to the customers that have been dumb enough to buy my Derivatives.

Let me briefly describe the type of Derivative that will become the most dangerous one for the coming Euro Crisis – the Interest Rate Swap.

<u>Example: Interest Rate Swap Derivative</u>

An Interest Rate Swap is based on a bond. Let's say I own a $1 Billion bond that pays 5% per year or $50 million in interest. However, I am concerned that because of inflation, this same type of bond will pay 7% if it is issued at the end of the year. Now I don't know for sure that the interest rate will be 7% at the end of the year. It will vary depending upon market conditions. Nevertheless, I am willing to enter into a Derivative contract with a Counter Party. I will guarantee the Counter Party $50 million in interest payments at the end of the year. In return, the Counter Party will pay me the year end interest rate on $1 Billion. If this interest rate is 7%, then I win ($70 million – $50 million = $20 million in profit for me). If the interest rate is 2%, then I lose ($50 million – 20 million = $30 million in loss). This is the essence of an Interest Rate Swap Derivative. A fixed end (the fixed rate of interest) is swapped for the variable end (the market interest rate at the end of the year).

Why will this type of Derivative be so dangerous to the Eurozone? I will explain that later. Before I do so, I will spend the next Chapter describing some of the important characteristics of Derivatives.

Summary

This Chapter is simply to illustrate that there are many types of Derivatives. The intent is not to make you a Derivative expert. The heart of a true Derivative is "risk transfer". The next Chapter will deal with more characteristics of Derivatives.

Addendum

I list plenty of books in the Bibliography which the reader can get more information on Derivatives.

Chapter 10. Derivative Characteristics

Derivatives are lucrative

Among other things, I used to sell real estate. The least expensive house I sold was $200,000 and the most expensive was $1,400,000. The commission on both was 3%. The difficulty in selling each house was about the same, but the commission was dramatically different. It was $6,000 for the $200,000 house and $42,000 for the $1,400,000 house. This phenomena ($6,000 vs. $42,000) is sometimes described as "scalability". In other words, even if your commission is a measly 2% but you sell $600 Trillion of Derivatives, this comes out to a nice, tidy $12 Trillion which is my estimate of what the Derivative makers have made during the past decade. Are Derivatives the golden goose that keeps laying golden eggs? It is the super golden goose. Derivative makers want to continue to keep their Derivatives secret and unregulated. They want to keep the general Public ignorant and confused (and they have succeeded).

Derivatives are unregulated

Unregulated Mortgage Backed Derivatives contributed mightily to the Subprime Crisis. Why weren't they regulated? Well, there was an attempt to do this, and it failed. Brooksley Born, head of the CFTC in the late 1990s, tried to regulate Derivatives. Her effort was quashed by the Secretary of the Treasury Rubin (former head of Goldman Sachs), Fed Chairman Alan Greenspan and Larry Summers (until recently the head of the Council of Economic Advisors). But don't take my word for it. Go and buy the DVD from PBS that tells the whole story (www.pbs.org, go to "shop", search for "The

Warning"). Talk about a fork in the road. If Mortgage Backed Derivatives had been regulated in the 1990s, we probably wouldn't have had the 2008 Panic and 10% unemployment. We still would have had a recession.

Note: When I say that Derivatives are unregulated, I am referring to the 98% of all Derivatives that are not regulated by the CFTC. The Dodd Frank Bill which purports to regulate Derivatives does virtually nothing. Derivatives remain unregulated.

Derivatives are SECRET

The principal reason why almost no one understands Derivatives is that they are *SECRET*. If you want to know the price of GE stock, simply turn on your computer or look at your TV financial show, and you will see the publically traded price of GE. However, if you want to know the price of a particular Mortgage Backed Security, good luck. This information is more secret than the identity of CIA agents. The trades of these and other Derivatives are handled in Dark Pools which are exchanges between two parties facilitated by our biggest banks. The lack of a public price for Mortgage Backed Securities is one of the major reasons that the Subprime losses turned a Recession into a Panic. No one knew what the values of these convoluted Mortgage Derivatives were so they imagined the worse. A $200 Billion [10-1] Subprime loss morphed into a $5 Trillion Toxic Monster as depicted in Figure 10-1. The term used for these Secret Mortgage Derivatives was opaque. What that really means is that these Derivative makers that extol the virtues of "no regulation" and the "free marketplace" really want a Secret marketplace. They don't want CFTC visibility.

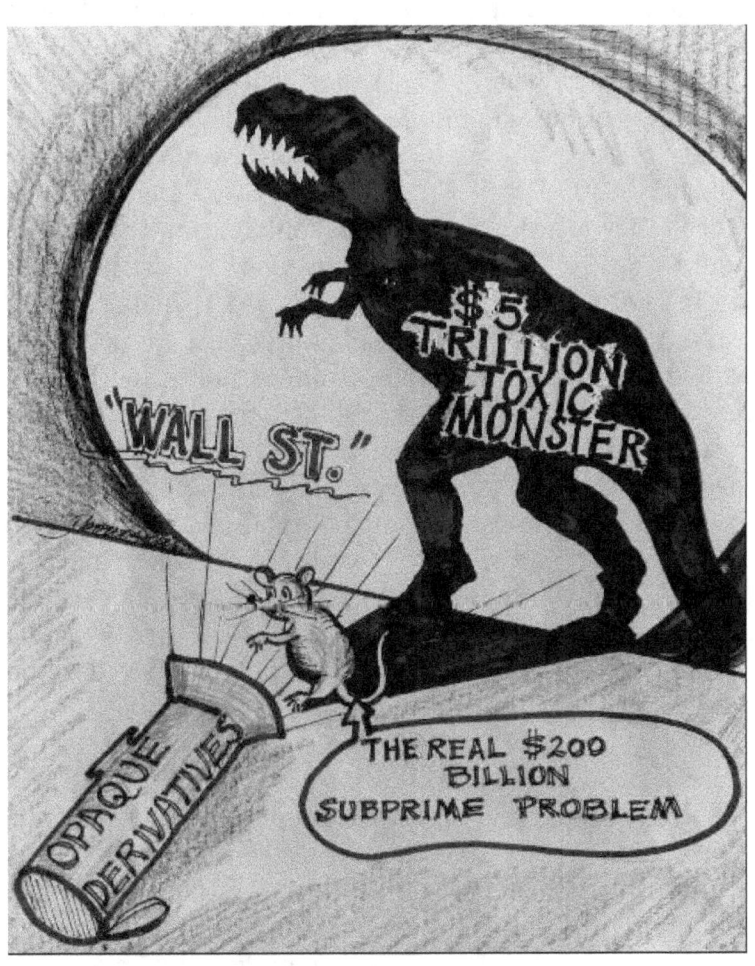

Figure 10 -1. Derivatives magnified the Subprime Problem

Derivatives are so SECRET they're not on Balance Sheets
Let me give an example. AIG was the world's largest insurance company with a $1 Trillion Balance Sheet. This refers to the approximately $1 Trillion that it held in Assets. Its Liabilities were just slightly less than $1 Trillion. However, what was missing from its Liabilities section was the approximately $400 Bil of Credit Default Swap Derivatives it had issued. If you were an AIG stockholder, don't you think you would want to know that AIG could be on the hook for paying off $400 Bil in Credit Default Swap (CDS) claims? As it turned out, AIG couldn't pay its claims or post the necessary collateral so the day after Lehman Brothers failed, the Federal Reserve took it over with $180 Bil of US taxpayer money. This is about 180 Billion reasons why you should learn about Derivatives. Taxpayers are paying for the Balance Sheet invisibility of Derivatives. The actual total of all Derivatives held by AIG at the time of its demise was $2.5 Trillion, none of which was shown on its Balance Sheet [10-2]. Another example is Lehman. At the time of its demise, it had approximately $600 Billion of assets. It also had a mind boggling $39 Trillion of Derivatives (not in its Liabilities section).

Has our financial market ever suffered from Balance Sheet abuse before? Sure. Enron was a prime case. One of the tricks they did was to take items off their Balance Sheets before year end and then put them back on the Balance Sheet in the early months of the next year. These selective accounting omissions resulted in a thorough accounting investigation, the Sarbanes-Oxley Act and the demise of Anderson Accounting. The accounting abuse by Enron (roughly a $60 Bil bankruptcy) was only a fraction of the $180 Bil accounting omission by

AIG and its accountants. Yet this huge accounting omission has not been investigated at all!

Derivatives are Dangerous

The AIG case described very briefly above is an example of the danger of Derivatives. The world's largest insurance company was essentially bankrupted by Credit Default Swap Derivatives. Opaque Mortgage Backed Derivatives were at the heart of the Wall St. bank failures and near failures. The Orange County bankruptcy (described later) is another example of the danger of Derivatives. The type of Derivative in the case of Orange County was the Interest Rate Swap Derivative which is the main focus of Part 3 of this book.

Derivatives do not contribute to economic growth

Good Derivatives "transfer risk". Bad Derivatives (90% of all Derivatives) are merely gambling devices (as I will explain in the next Chapter). Neither type of Derivative contributes to economic growth nor will ever create a single additional job.

Let's consider the "Good" Airline Oil Futures Contract. This Derivative will give the airline a type of oil price insurance, but it will not contribute to growth. Do you know of any book on economics that says the best way to stimulate an economy is to buy more insurance? If the airline were to add another airplane to its fleet, it would be adding to economic growth. It would probably create new jobs.

Just visualize your Fire Insurance on your home. If you doubled the amount of insurance would you create economic growth? No.

Observation.
No book on Economics I have ever read says that the way to stimulate economic growth and create jobs is to buy more insurance. How much economic growth has come from $600 Trillion of Derivatives??

Let's say you have $1 Bil and use it to develop a new computer. You are "adding economic value" with the new computer. You are probably also creating new jobs because people have to design and build your new computer. Derivatives don't add economic value or create new jobs. On a good day, Derivatives "transfer risk". On a bad day, Derivatives are simply a gambling tool. Does an increase in gambling increase economic growth? On neither a good or bad day do Derivatives contribute anything to economic growth (unless you count the big commissions as growth).

Summary
Hopefully the discussion of the past two Chapters has given you the reader some basic understanding of Derivatives. In Chapter 9, I briefly discussed several types of Derivatives (not all types). In Chapter 10, I discussed how Derivatives are lucrative, unregulated, Secret, not on Balance Sheets and are dangerous. At best, a good Derivative can "transfer risk". This has nothing to do with economic growth or adding jobs which is not a ringing endorsement of the $600 Trillion Derivative market. At worst, Derivatives have morphed into gambling devices.

Chapter 11. Synthetic Derivatives & Gambling

"Investment risk" vs. "gambling risk"
The essence of capitalism is to invest money (capital) to develop a new product. In other words, investors may put money into Apple Computer Company to build a new computer. The end product of a capitalistic investment is to produce something that "adds value". Are investors assured of success in any such venture? No. They could lose all of their money. Their investment has a "risk" associated with it. For those people with a short circuit in their logic, gambling is just the same as the capitalistic investment I have described above. Just like the capital investment, gambling also has "risk". Therefore investments and gambling are the same. Here is why that logic utterly fails. In gambling, there is nothing of value that is ever produced. You can play 1,000 games of poker or spin the roulette wheel 1,000 times. You might actually win money, but nothing of value is ever produced from poker or roulette wheels. Let me try to state this in a different way:

Investment = risk + value added
Gambling = risk

Gambling obviously will never produce anything of economic value for our economy or create any new jobs. It's simply a bet that has risk associated with it. Approximately 90% of the

$600 Trillion Derivative market is nothing more than gambling. Our US and Eurozone banks both create and own these Derivatives. They shouldn't.

Good Derivatives can change into gambling bets if there is no "risk transfer". Let me give some examples:

Example: Oil Futures Contracts morphs into a bet

In the earlier example, an airline which had risk exposure to rising oil prices purchased an oil futures contract from a Counter Party. It transferred its risk of higher oil prices to the Counter Party. This serves an economic purpose for the airline.

Now let's switch the party purchasing the oil futures contract to a Hedge Fund. The Hedge Fund has no risk exposure to rising oil prices. The Hedge Fund is merely using the oil futures contract to bet that it is smarter than the Counter Party in predicting which way oil prices will go. If oil prices go up, the Hedge Fund wins. If oil prices go down, the Counter Party wins. It is simply a bet and pure gambling. It might as well have been a bet of the Steelers vs. the Packers in the Superbowl (which would also have no economic purpose).

Example: Fire Insurance on my house becomes a bet

I own a house. I transfer the risk of it burning down to an Insurance Company. This is a legitimate economic risk transfer.

However, if my neighbor owns the fire insurance on my house, this fire insurance contract has changed into a bet. My neighbor is betting that my house will burn down and is willing to pay a premium to the Insurance Company to get the full payout if it does burn down. However, my neighbor is exposed to no risk if my house burns down.

Now Fire Insurance is not a Derivative, but it is a good example of how a good risk transfer contract can change into an economically worthless bet. There is no legitimate risk transfer.

In the above example, my neighbor bought insurance on my house. This couldn't happen in the insurance industry because it is regulated by State Insurance Commissioners that insist on the party buying insurance having an "Insurable Interest". In other words, you must own what you buy insurance on (which sort of makes sense).

Example: Abacus CDO [11-1] and its Credit Default Swap

In the world of Derivatives this doesn't apply since there is absolutely no regulation. The famous Abacus Subprime CDO (a type of Derivative) is a great example of this. The Abacus CDO ($1 Billion) was created by Goldman Sachs and sold to German Bank IKB. Within 6 months, it was essentially worthless. Goldman later settled with the SEC and paid a $500 Million fine. However, the aspect of the Abacus case that I want to discuss concerned the Credit Default Swap (CDS) on the Abacus CDO for $1 Billion which provided insurance in the event of the Abacus CDO failure. If German Bank IKB had purchased this CDS then when its Abacus CDO dropped to zero value, it would have been fully compensated. However, this is not what happened. While the German Bank IKB had an insurable interest, the CDS on Abacus was sold to the Paulson Hedge Fund which had no risk associated with Abacus. When the Abacus CDO lost its value, the Paulson Hedge Fund received a $1 Billion payout. The Paulson Hedge Fund had merely used the CDS Derivative as a bet against the Abacus CDO. It had merely made a small premium payment (probably less than $10 Million) and made a cool $1 Billion. Every gambler in Las Vegas would admire this.

Essentially what the Paulson Hedge Fund did was similar to buying Fire Insurance on my house and then collecting the payout when it burned down. This isn't capitalism. It's gambling.

The "Risk Transfer" Test

The essential test as to whether a Derivative serves a useful economic function is whether or not it has one party that is transferring risk. ***If there is no "risk transfer", the Derivative is simply a gambling device.*** It is simply a bet. It belongs in Las Vegas and not in the middle of our financial system.

All Synthetic Derivatives fail the "risk transfer" test. All of them are simply gambling devices. What is a Synthetic Derivative? Let me explain the concept with my familiar example of Fire Insurance.

> **Example: Synthetic Fire Insurance**
> I own Fire Insurance on my house. This is a legitimate economic transfer of risk. However, if my neighbor owns an additional Fire Insurance policy on my house, this is a synthetic Fire Insurance contract. If 10 more people in New York also own Fire Insurance contracts on my house, those contracts are also "Synthetic".

How many Synthetic Derivatives are there? Most of the $600 Trillion of Derivatives are Synthetic. Let me illustrate with Interest Rate Swaps.

> **Synthetic Interest Rate Swaps**
> There are $400 Trillion of Interest Rate Swaps. These Interest Rate Swaps could derive from private corporate bonds or government bonds. I would estimate the US corporate bond market at roughly $10 Billion and the US government bond market at roughly $10 Billion as well. This would total $20 Billion in bonds. If I estimate that Europe has roughly the same amount of bonds, I have a worldwide total of $40 Trillion. If there were a one to one correlation between real world bonds and Interest Rate Swaps, there would be $40 Trillion of Interest Rate Swaps. Yet, there are 10 times this amount or $400 Trillion. This can only happen because most of the Interest Rate Swaps are Synthetic or copies of real world Interest Rate Swaps. Most Interest Rate Swaps are Synthetic.

There are a couple of important conclusions that can be drawn from this:

(1) There is a huge amount of gambling going on in the world of Derivatives.

(2) If there are real world losses in bonds, these losses could be multiplied by a factor of 10 due to Synthetic Derivatives. This is going to affect the Eurozone in a big way.

Let's go back to my Example of Synthetic Fire Insurance. Let's say my house is worth $400,000. If my house burns down, the Insurance Company will have to pay me $400,000. However, let's say that additionally there are 10 Synthetic Fire Insurance Contracts on my house. Now if my house burns down, the Fire Insurance Company will have to pay a total of $4,400,000 instead of merely $400,000. This is why Synthetic Derivatives [11-2] are so absolutely dangerous. They multiply real world losses. This is what is about to happen in the Eurozone.

Note: Now, of course, I am just considering the loss side of the equation. The Insurance Company is going to lose big time, but the 10 Synthetic Insurance Contract owners in New York will win $4,000,000. While this may comfort some, it doesn't comfort me. If Eurozone banks are on the losing end of Interest Rate Swap contracts, they will probably go bankrupt. It is small comfort if some Hedge Funds in New York are big winners at their expense.

Chapter 12. Interest Rate Swap Derivatives

The Interest Rate Swap Derivative market is over $400 Trillion in size. This dwarfs the US GDP of $15 Trillion or the Eurozone GDP of $12 Trillion. Just the size alone of this Derivative market suggests that every person should know something about it. Although I have briefly described Interest Rate Swaps, since they are so central to the coming Euro Crisis, I want to go over them in more detail in this Chapter.

Example of an Interest Rate Swap Derivative
An Interest Rate Swap Derivative is derived from a bond. Let's say you own a $1 Bil bond that pays 3% interest per year or $30 million in interest. However, you think that in the year ahead there will be inflation and interest rates will go up. Let's say you believe that the interest rate on a bond with a risk level like yours will pay 5% interest. Effectively, you will lose 2% interest. No problem. A Derivative maker will create an Interest Rate Swap Derivative that will let you exchange (or swap) your fixed 3% interest for a variable interest rate which will be determined by what happens in the market.

Definition: Interest Rate Swap Derivative
This Derivative is based on the fixed interest rate of a specific bond which is swapped (or exchanged) for the actual (or variable) market rate of a comparable benchmark interest rate at the end of 1 year (or some fixed time period). The actual market rate will, of course, be a *variable* interest rate depending on market conditions.

What is a "comparable benchmark interest rate"? Let's say that the reference bond is a 5 year US Treasury bond issued in Jan 2010. The "comparable benchmark interest rate" would be a 5 year US Treasury bond issued in Jan 2011. Let's say that in Jan 2010, the 5 year US Treasury bond was issued at a 3% interest rate, but in Jan 2011 the 5 year Treasury bond was issued at 5% interest rate. It is the same type of bond, but the interest rate has changed because the inflation environment has changed.

The example of a government benchmark interest rate above is very simple. For a company's bond, it is more likely that an interest rate like LIBOR (London Interbank Offer Rate) will be used. In fact, it would probably be something like Libor + 4%. In the case of a variable rate mortgage, some reference interest rate + 4% or some amount is used. This is similar to Interest Rate Swaps.

The first important observation that should be made about Interest Rate Swaps is that there are two ends to the contract: (1) The party at one end agrees to pay a fixed interest rate (e.g., 3% in the above example), (2) The party at the other end agrees to pay the variable interest rate prevailing at the end of the contract period.

Interest Rate Swap – Fixed End and Variable End
There are two ends of an Interest Rate Swap contract. The party on the fixed end agrees to pay a fixed rate of interest (3% in the above example) while the party on the variable end agrees to pay the variable market interest rate at the end of the time period. Which is the dangerous end of the contract? It is

> the variable end. If interest rates spike upward, there is no limit to possible losses.

The second important observation that should be made about Interest Rate Swaps is that they are quoted in Notional Value. In the above example the Notional Value is $1 Billion. Does this mean that the party buying the Interest Rate Swap Derivative paid $1 Billion? No. The buyer would pay only a small percentage of the value of the bond such as 1%.

Notional Value of an Interest Rate Swap
The Notional Value of an Interest Rate Swap is the value of the bond in question. However, the Interest Rate Swap only deals with the variation between the fixed interest rate and variable interest rates associated with that bond.

Whew. When I compared the value of the Interest Rate Swap Derivative market of $400 Trillion with the US GDP of $15 Trillion that comparison was worrisome. Since the $400 Trillion is just Notional Value, maybe the situation is not so bad. Not quite.

In the above example, $1 Billion was the Notional Value, but the difference between 5% and 3% is merely $20 million in interest payments. That doesn't seem so bad. Unfortunately, if the whole interest rate market is affected, it can be. If the entire $400 Trillion market were merely affected by the same 2% rise in interest rate, this would result in payments of $8 Trillion (0.02 x $400 Tril = $8 Tril). No banking system in the world has that kind of money. Thus, there is reason for concern.

Interest Rate Swap Derivatives correlation with reality

Do I believe that the $400 Tril Interest Rate Swap Derivative market is seriously flawed? Absolutely yes. In the example above, I correlated a 5 year US Treasury bond with one Interest Rate Swap Derivative. Is there anything wrong with this? As long as the payer of the variable interest rate end has the money to pay, there is no problem. There is a one to one correlation between a real world bond and a single Derivative. The slip from logic to sophistry comes when many Derivatives are keyed off the same bond.

Estimated Size of the World Bond Market - $40 Tril

I will make a Ball Park estimate of the size of the world bond market. The US stock market is $10 Tril and as a first estimate, I will guess the US bond market for private companies is also $10 Tril. As a first estimate, I will guess that our US government bond market is also $10 Tril for a total $20 Tril of US bonds. I will estimate the EU private and national bond market at the same size -- $20 Tril. This would give a worldwide bond market of approximately $40 Trillion.

Now some may quibble with my estimate, but I will claim that they are concerned with 2nd order effects. Since not all readers are mathematicians, let me explain the difference between 1st and 2nd order effects.

1ˢᵗ and 2ⁿᵈ order effects

Let's say I have a number, 402. If I change the digit in the hundreds position by increasing it by 5, my number changes to 902. This is a huge change. It is a 1ˢᵗ order effect. If I change the digit in the tens position by 5, my number changes to 452. This is a 2ⁿᵈ order effect.

My point is this: If the world bond market is truly $30 Tril or as high as $50 Tril, it is a 2ⁿᵈ order effect compared to the $400 Trillion Interest Rate Swap Derivative market.

Key Question:

How can the Interest Rate Swap Derivative market be $400 Trillion when the real world bond market is only $40 Trillion?

The answer is that most (about 90%) of the Interest Rate Swap market is synthetic or artificial. If you have forgotten what a "synthetic derivative" is, please go back to the previous Chapter and review this concept. It is absolutely essential to understand.

Please recall my example with Fire Insurance. If the value of all houses in the US is $10 Trillion (approximately the correct value), then one would logically expect that there could be no more than $10 Trillion in fire insurance. If someone told you that the value of fire insurance was $100 or $200 Trillion, you would say that something is very fishy. This is exactly the case with Interest Rate Swaps.

How can this financial travesty occur? The principal reason is that there is absolutely no regulation of Interest Rate Swaps in the US or EU. In the US, the pathetic Dodd bill exempted Interest Rate Swaps from regulation because they are "safe". A second reason why Interest Rate Swaps are larger than their real world bond counterparts is that they are secret and invisible. They don't appear in the Liabilities section of any bank's Balance Sheet. It is like Gaddafi's anti-aircraft guns trying to shoot down a stealth plane that they can't see. If you can't see it, it is tough to shoot. Furthermore, these Interest Rate Swaps do not trade on public exchanges where everyone can see the trading prices as well as determine the size of the market.

Chapter 13. Derivative Triggers

In the Wall St. Panic of 2008, Subprime Derivatives failed dramatically, but Interest Rate Swaps did not fail at all. If both of these types of Derivatives went through the same economic downturn, why didn't both fail? The answer is that it takes a ***different financial event to trigger*** the failure of different types of Derivatives.

The Trigger for Subprime Derivative Failures
During normal times, the failure rate for conventional mortgages is about 1%. During recessions, this can increase to 5%. Subprime mortgages are much riskier. During normal times, they probably have a 5% failure rate. However, during the first recession these Subprimes faced (the 2008 Recession), the failure rate was catastrophic. Some data indicates a 35% failure rate by 2007. Since 2008 was an even worse year, I estimate that the cumulative failure rate for Subprime mortgages is probably above 75%.

Subprime Derivative Trigger
The trigger for Subprime Derivative failures was the real estate market prices finally going down after a steady 10 year rise upward. The drop in real estate prices caused a catastrophic failure rate in the flawed Subprime mortgages.

The Figures below show that when real estate prices went down in 2008, the failures of Subprimes just shot up dramatically (also in 2008). (The Figures are just representative and not an attempt to present accurate data.)

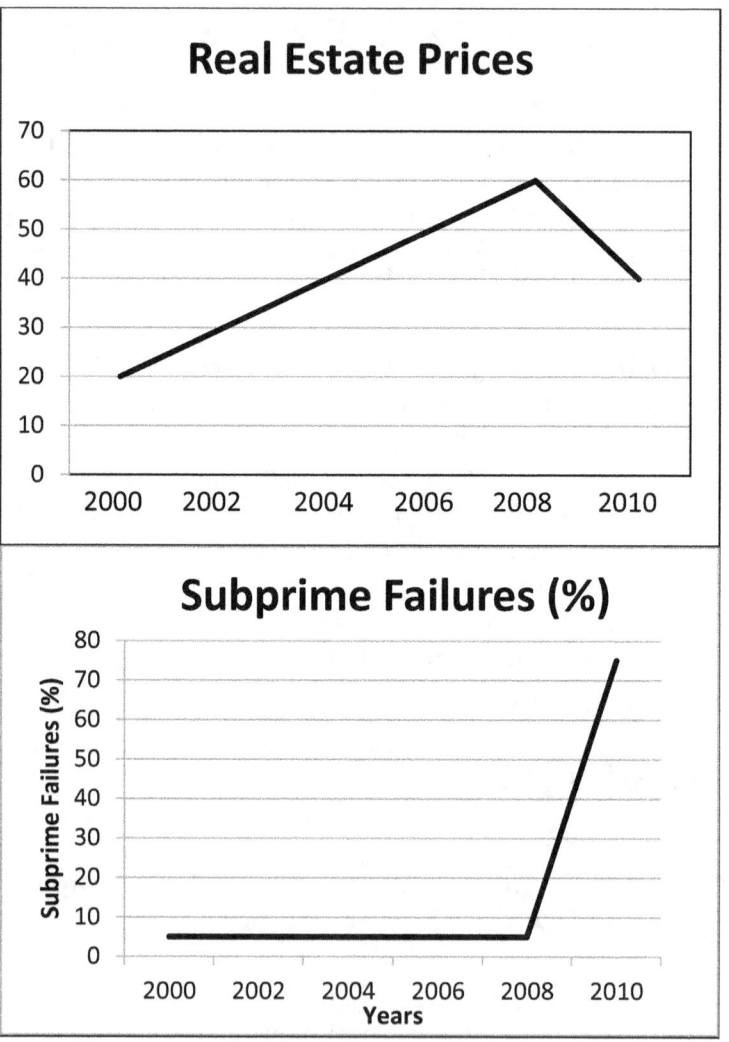

Figure 13.1 Subprime Trigger 2008

Again, what the Figures above show is that the downward turn in real estate prices *__triggered__* and upward spike in Subprime failures.

The Trigger for Interest Rate Swaps

Interest rates have been relatively benign [13-1] for the 2000-2011 time period. Generally, they have been 3% + or − 2% for the most part. The amount of interest rate change during a 1 year period is really more important than the interest level as far as Interest Rate Swaps are concerned. The interest rate change along with the size of the Interest Rate Swaps affected will determine the size of the Interest Rate Swap losses.

Interest Rate Swap Losses

(Interest Rate Change) x (amount of Swaps) = Losses
    5% (or 0.05)   x $20 Trillion   = $1 Trillion

What is the Trigger for Interest Rate Swap losses? It is an *__upward spike__* in interest rates during a relatively short period of time (e.g., 1 year). By spike, I mean a rapid rise in interest rates that remains high (i.e., a new higher plateau). I do not mean a spike that lasts only 1 week. If interest rates have nominally been 3% for the last decade, then they can only spike 3% downward. *__The danger is with an upward interest rate spike which can be unlimited.__*

Interest Rate Swap Trigger

A significant (e.g., 5%) upward spike in interest rates will cause huge Interest Rate Swap losses.

I want to try and illustrate the concept of an Interest Rate Swap Trigger both with a Table and with Figures. See note [13-1].

Table 13-1. Interest Rate Changes and Swap Losses

Year	Interest Rate Chg	Swap Amount ($ Bil)	Swap Losses ($ Bil)
2000	1	10,000	100
2001	4	10,000	400
2002	1	10,000	100
2003	0	10,000	0
2004	1	10,000	100
2005	2	10,000	200
2006	1	20,000	200
2007	1	20,000	200
2008	3	20,000	600 covered by TARP
2009	0	20,000	0
2010	0	20,000	0
2011	0	20,000	0
2012	7	20,000	1,400 Interest Rate Spike Trigger

Column 1 is the interest rate ***change*** not the absolute interest rate. Column 2 is an estimate of the amount of Interest Rate Swaps involved, and Column 3 is the loss resulting from multiplying Column 1 by 2. The 7% spike is in year 2012. Figure 13.2 below shows this same information in chart form.

Figure 13.2 Interest Rate Swap Losses

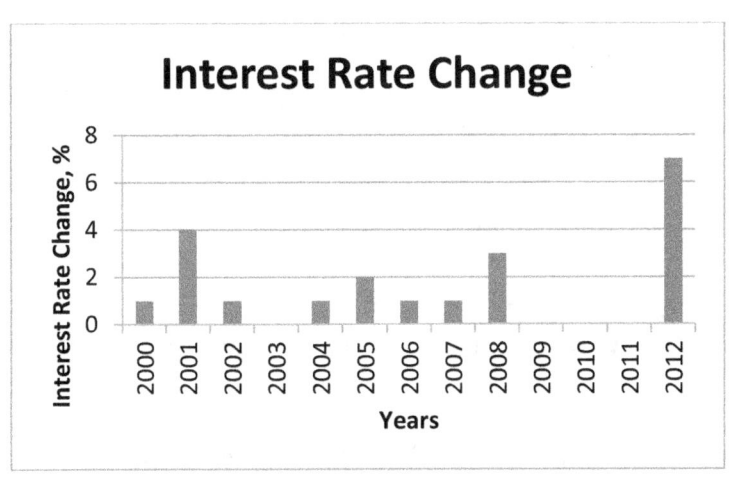

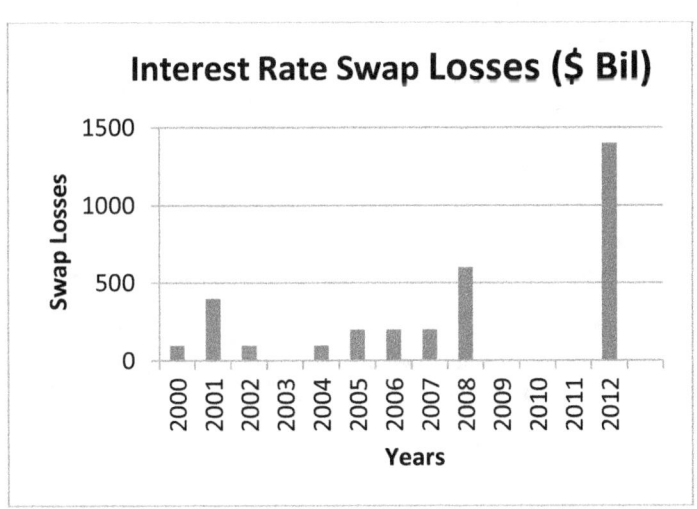

Summary

Derivative Triggers	
Derivative	Trigger
Subprime	Real Estate Prices go down
Interest Rate Swap	Interest Rate Spike upward

We have seen the Subprime Derivative trigger in action, and the results were devastating. We have yet to see the Interest Rate Swap Derivative Trigger in action. We will.

For the courageous, please read Appendix 6 on Triggers.

Chapter 14. Interest Rate Swap Losses

It is extremely difficult to make any kind of meaningful estimate of what Interest Rate Swap Losses might be for the Eurozone. Let me start with a real world example where we do know the size of the interest rate spike and approximately the size of the Interest Rate Swaps involved.

Real World Example: The Orange County Bankruptcy [14-1]
In the 1990s, the Treasurer of Orange County, California tried to make some money for his county government. Instead of merely putting his money in a bank or in T-Bills, he invested in Interest Rate Swaps. He thought he could predict the direction of interest rates. Initially, he was successful and made some money for the county. However, in 1994 he guessed that interest rates were headed down while the Fed raised them 3%. This *3% interest rate rise* was enough to *trigger* a $2 Billion bankruptcy for the county. School budgets were cut. Libraries closed etc. It was a small example of what Interest Rate Swap losses can mean. It was a $2 Billion loss on $20 Billion of investments (not all Interest Rate Swaps).

Let me use the Orange County case to illustrate the required elements, and the formula that is needed to determine Interest Rate Swap Losses. Then I will make my assumptions about these elements for the Eurozone and use the formula to come up with an estimated loss of $1 Trillion.

> **Required Elements for EU Interest Rate Swap Losses**
> For Eurozone banks to suffer significant Interest Rate Swap losses, there are 3 essential elements:
>
> **1. "Variable End".** The banks must hold the "variable" end of the Interest Rate Swaps.
> **2. Amount of Swaps.** The banks must hold a significant amount of Interest Rate Swaps (i.e., $Trillions).
> **3. Interest Rate Spike.** There must be a significant upward interest rate spike greater than the normal +/- 2% fluctuation.

Orange County held the "variable end" of Interest Rate Swaps. The amount was approximately $20 Billion. Orange County suffered a 3% Interest Rate Spike. What is the formula for calculating Interest Rate Swap Losses?

> **Formula for Interest Rate Swap Losses**
> The formula for determining the amount of Eurozone Interest Rate Swap Losses is pretty simple:
>
> **(Interest Rate Spike) x (amount of Swaps) = Losses**
>
> For example:
>
> **5% (or 0.05) x $20 Trillion = $1 Trillion in losses**

The difficulty is the exact determination of the size of the interest rate spike and size of the Derivatives affected. For the Eurozone, let me discuss those elements and my assumptions further.

1. "Variable End [14-2]"

Do I know which Eurozone banks hold the "variable' end of Interest Rate Swaps and the total value of those Derivatives? No I don't. I am no better off than my Physics professor knowing how many barbers there are in the US. I will have to make a reasoned estimate based on the knowledge available to me. Does the ECB know which banks hold the variable end of Interest Rate Swaps and what the total value of these Derivatives are? I doubt it. I just don't think the ECB understands Derivatives any more than our Fed does. However, if the ECB was on the ball, they could go to every Eurozone bank and find this information out. I surely hope they do so. If the ECB knows the size of the Derivatives then it is a simple matter of assuming various sized interest rate spikes to determine possible losses.

2. Amount of Interest Rate Swaps [14-3]

What is the size of the Interest Rate Swap Derivatives held by Eurozone banks that will be affected? The ECB can come up with an exact number, but I will have to make an estimate. The entire worldwide Interest Rate Swap market is $400 Trillion, and I estimate that $200 Trillion is keyed off Eurozone bonds. However, I am going to dramatically reduce the amount that will affect Eurozone banks to a mere $20 Trillion. In the interest of trying to keep this book at as simple a level as possible, I will merely state my assumption of $20 Trillion, but I will give some further rationale for this in Appendix 6. (Note: Please recall that a single US bank, Lehman, held $39 Trillion of Derivatives by itself.)

Assumption 1. Size of Eurozone Interest Rate Swaps

I assume that the size of the Interest Rate Swaps affecting the Eurozone is $20 Trillion of the $400 Trillion market.

---

3. Interest Rate Spike

Do I or the ECB have any idea what the size of an interest rate spike would be in the event of a Greek Default? No. We have to estimate. If we look at the Greek bonds in the secondary market, their interest rates have gone up from roughly 3% to 28% in a year. Similarly, Irish and Portuguese bonds have gone up from 3% to 12% in a year. This indicates that a Eurozone interest rate spike(s) could be quite large. If we even look at relatively stable British bonds, we can see that there was a 6% interest rate rise in 1988 without even a Default involved.

As I have noted, the past decade has seen relatively stable, benign interest rates that have varied no more the 2% during a year. A spike would be something that would exceed this range of normal fluctuation. For example, if interest rates rose a total of 7%, this would be 5% above the normal range of fluctuation

---

Assumption 2. Interest Rate Spike due to a Greek Default

I assume 5%.

Based on Assumptions 1 & 2, I can make an estimate of Interest Rate Swap Losses to the Eurozone following a Greek Default.

Estimated Eurozone Losses from Interest Rate Swaps
(Interest Rate Spike) x (Size of Swaps) = Losses   5%   x $20 Trillion   = ***$1 Trillion***

Reality or a Wild Guess (WAG)

In Part 2, I presented my estimated range for the PIG Defaults of $500-900 Billion. Now I am presenting an even larger estimate of Derivative Losses that will be part of the fallout of these Defaults. Is this just a Wild Guess?

If I were to present my Part 3 as part of a PhD thesis, it would be rejected. I haven't proven anything. But the Pilot in me says that with $400 Trillion of Interest Rate Swaps out there, it is better to make a WAG than simply avoid the problem as Economists would do. The Pilot in me says that there is going to be an Interest Rate Spike when Greece defaults. That Interest Rate Spike, and the net position (see Appendix 6) of Interest Rate Swaps held by Eurozone banks is going to mean huge additional losses piled on top of already huge Default losses.

Am I right or wrong? If the brain dead ECB continues with its Magic level thinking (i.e., Greece will not default), then we are likely to find out the hard way that I was closer to the truth than those who claim Interest Rate Swaps are safe.

Part 4. Growth

Chapter 15. Growth – more work

In Part 4, I am going to discuss one of the missing elements in the discussions on what to do in the Euro Crisis --- more economic growth. Certainly every European Economist wishes for growth, but it just doesn't fall from a tree. You have to earn it. Two ways of generating more growth are: (1) work more and (2) innovate more. This Chapter will look at some ways that Europeans can work more. Here are 3 simple examples illustrating what growth can and cannot do.

Example 1. Shrinking the National Debt using growth
Country A starts with a National Debt = its GDP which means its National Debt is 100% GDP. But Country A consistently grows at 5% GDP each year for 10 years with Budget Deficits – 0. At year 10, its National Debt has shrunk to 67% GDP. Note: The Nat Debt remains $100 Bil throughout all 10 years.

Table 15-1 Shrinking National Debt as a % GDP			
Year	Country A GDP	Country A National Debt	Nat Debt As % GDP
1	$100 Bil	$100 Bil	100%
2	$105 Bil	$100 Bil	95
3	$110 Bil	$100 Bil	91
.	.	.	.
.	.	.	.
10	$150 Bil	$100 Bil	67

The astute observer will note that I really didn't use 5% growth compounded yearly but simply a $5 Bil increase yearly in GDP. This is good enough for a quick Ball Park analysis which shows that *if the Budget Deficit can be zeroed out and Country A can grow at 5%*, it can shrink its National Debt down to a manageable 67% of GDP. Growth is powerful.

Example 2. Eurozone Growth at 5%
If the Eurozone could grow at 5% for just one year, its growth would be $600 Bil (i.e., 0.05 x $12 Tril = $600 Bil). This $600 Bil could handle the estimated Defaults of all three PIG countries. The EU could move past its Euro Crisis and on to better things. Just one year of vigorous growth could solve the Euro Crisis. Growth is powerful.

Example 3. Will 5% growth save Greece?
Unfortunately the answer is No. It will help. Let me go back to what I consider the most important table in the book which predicts the Greeks will run out of bailout funds in early 2012.

Table 6-3. How long does the Bailout Fund last for Greece?				
Year	Begin Bailout	Rollover Required	Budget Deficit	End Bailout
½ 2010	143	-21	-23	99
2011	99	-43	-33	23
2012	23	-43	-33	-53 (**Default**)
½ 2013	-53	-21	-17	-91

Table 15-2 below shows what growth of 5% GDP means for Greece. All 5% of the growth does not go into increasing the tax revenue. However, the Greek tax rate (personal + Value

Added Tax) is about 50% so half of the growth will go into more tax revenue (labeled More Tax). The results are:

Table 15-2. Greece grows 5% GDP each year				
Year	GDP	5% GDP	Cum Growth	More Tax
2011	$330 Bil	$16 Bil	$16	$ 8 Bil
2012	$346 Bil	$17 Bil	$33	$17 Bil
½ 2013	$363 Bil	$18 Bil	$51	$12 Bil

Note: Each year's growth adds to next year's. I cut the growth in half for More Tax revenue except for 2013 because the bailout funds run out halfway through 2013. Also, I did not include an End of year GDP. This is simply the same as the beginning GDP for the next year.

Now I modify Table 6-3 by adding a column for More Tax revenue (the white column in the above Table):

Table 6-3. How long does the Bailout Fund last for Greece?					
Year	Begin Bailout	Rollover Required	Budget Deficit	More Tax	End Bailout
½ 2010	143	-21	-23		99
2011	99	-43	-33	8	23
2012	23	-43	-33	17	-36 (**Default**)
½ 2013	-36	-21	-17	12	-62

The sad result for Greece is that it will still run out of Bailout funds in 2012 before its 3 year mark of June 2013. What this says to Greece is that while growth is helpful, Greek needs are near term and can really only be addressed by also zeroing out its Budget Deficit.

<u>Growth is a long term panacea and not a short term one</u>
The message for the PIG countries is that they should strive for
more growth. It will help them in the long run. However, the
beneficial effects of growth will not be enough to help them in
the short run. Only draconian Budget cuts are going to get the
job done.

However, for the Eurozone as a whole, the message is a little
different. If the Eurozone weren't suffering from Eurosclerosis
growth of 1% per year, it could easily handle the PIG Defaults.
However, since it has such poor growth it would take a half a
decade of growth to pay for the $500 Bil PIG Defaults. The
European attitude about their Welfare States is "Who needs
growth when we have cradle to grave care, long vacations and
a relaxed lifestyle. Let the dumb Americans have their Rat
Race in the pursuit of growth."

<u>Pie Dividers and Pie Makers</u>
My wife is a TV food network junkie so I explained the
difference between the Welfare States of Europe vs. Capitalism
in terms of pies. The overarching aim of Welfare States is to
divide the pie between all people as evenly as possible. In US
Capitalism, it is to grow bigger and bigger pies. For example,
in France they do not have anyone as rich as Bill Gates of
Microsoft. Their personal income levels are more equal. Here
is the downside to that approach. France doesn't have
Microsoft either. If Bill Gates gets a bigger slice of the pie
than I do I'm not too concerned. He brought a big pie to the
party. The emphasis of Capitalism is pie building. The Soviet
Union had perhaps the most equal pie dividing, but the cost
was an economy that was pathetic.

The Euro Crisis is why Europe needs to re-orient its priorities towards growth. Europe brought the world the Industrial Revolution and vast material progress. But Europe has traded healthy growth for big government, long vacations and settled for Eurosclerosis growth. It turns out that this was a Faustian bargain. Now Europe desperately needs healthy economic growth to help the PIGs and PIIGS. It needs growth to save the Euro and prevent economic stagnation.

Growth through more work

At least two ways for a country to grow are: (1) more work and (2) more innovation. Of course, doing both is better. Let me just discuss "more work" with a couple of examples. I will discuss growth through innovation in the next Chapter.

US growth during WWII

The US GDP nearly doubled during WWII. Furthermore, the US did it the hard way. It took perhaps 20% of its most able workers and put them in military uniform. Despite this, the country's GDP still grew. How did this happen? There are at least two reasons: (1) Everyone worked 60 hours/week and (2) when Joe the Riveter went into the Army, Rosie the Riveter took his place. It's pretty simple. More work = more growth.

Economic Truth

More Work = More Growth

There was something else that was simple about US growth during WWII. It wasn't hard to figure out what to work on –

whatever the military needed. How about 50,000 planes, thousands of tanks and a hundred aircraft carriers? In short, no marketing research was required. In peacetime, it is a little different. Good marketing [15-1] is required. It is not simply "working more" but "working more on something the marketplace is willing to buy". Another way of saying this is: "Finding a need and filling it".

China's growth since the time of Deng
China has figured out what the marketplace wants to buy. I suspect that nearly all US clothes are now manufactured in China. Initially Chairman Mao tried all the wonderful Communist techniques from The Great Leap Forward to The Cultural Revolution. Fortunately for China he died, and Deng took over. He kept the one party Communist government but opened up the economic sector to free enterprise. The results have been an astounding 20 years of growth at 10% per year. China is now the 2nd largest economy in the world. More work = more growth, and China has found the markets.

Europe: More Work = More Growth?
If Europe does its market research homework (as Germany does), it could easily grow more by working more. Let me just provide two illustrations. In their generous Welfare States, Europeans get cushy 6 week vacations each year. I never did. In fact, I ended up my career working 7 days/week for 10 years with only Christmas Day off [15-2]. But then I am a Rat Race American. Most Americans get 2 weeks of vacation vs. the European 6 week vacation. If Europeans were willing to reduce their vacations to the American model, what might be the increase in economic growth?

> **Table 15-3. 6 week vacations reduced to 2 week vacations**
> If Europeans increased the amount of working weeks from 46 to 50, the potential economic growth could be 8.7%
>
> **50/46 = 1.087 or potentially 8.7% more growth**

Again, it is not simply a question of only "working more". The hard work of marketing research must be done to figure out what work the worldwide marketplace is willing to pay for. The Germans and Finns seem to be able to do this. The rest of the Eurozone is weaker. Here's another simple way for Europeans to "work more".

> **Table 15-4. 40 hours/week vs. 35 hours/week**
> The calculation is shown below:
>
> **40/35 = 1.14 or potentially 14% more growth**

Bailouts, Austerity Budgets and Growth
Nearly all of the Eurozone effort during the Euro Crisis seems to be focused on Bailouts and Austerity Budgets. What has escaped consideration is "working more". Maybe it is time to give "growth" a chance.

As an American, let me say that I think Europeans are **_lazy_**. Please don't talk to me about "working class" and "35 hour work week" in the same sentence. If Europeans simply restored their work ethic to American standards (or Max Weber standards), they could easily work their way out of this Euro Crisis instead of spinning towards a break-up of the Euro Zone and possibly a 2nd Great Depression.

Summary

Communist Credo

You pretend to work, and we'll pretend to pay you.
Result: Economic Mediocrity.

Welfare State Credo

You don't have to work hard.
Result: Anemic economic growth.

Thatcher's Credo

Socialism is great until you run out of other people's money.

Greek Corollary

Socialism is great until you run out of German money.

Economic Truth

More Work = More Growth

Verified by the US and China

Chapter 16. Growth - more innovation

Parts 2 (Defaults) and 3 (Derivatives) are certainly pessimistic. Am I a pessimist? No. I am absolutely an optimist. I think we have a positively bright future ahead of us......if we can get by the present US and EU financial mismanagement. I think science and technology can bring us a bright future.

"Why Europe"

"Why Europe" is an excellent book which I recommend everyone read. It asks the critical question of why Europe economically dominated the world for the 19th and early 20th centuries. Was it a better law system, better political system, better resources or what? In my opinion, the author comes to the right conclusion by focusing on the Industrial Revolution begun by Britain and asking why it happened there. I will paraphrase his results in the following four elements:

Table 16-1. The Critical Ingredients for Growth

1. Inquiring minds (e.g., Galileo [16-1])
2. Science, Math (e.g., Newton, Leibniz [16-1])
3. Experimental Method, Invention (e.g, Bacon, Watt)
4. Entrepreneurship

First, let me observe a couple of items that didn't make it to the final list:

1. Derivatives
2. Pie Dividing

Let me take a couple of digs at these loser items. Derivatives are the opposite of Entrepreneurship. At best some Derivatives are risk transfer and about 90% of all Derivatives are useless gambling devices. Imagine if that colossal amount of money were put into useful investments as was done during the Industrial Revolution. Or, consider Pie Dividing. Pie Dividing doesn't grow anything. It simply re-distributes money. If the Eurozone spent as much time on growth as it does on Pie Dividing, it would have a healthy economic growth rate and more pie to divide.

Growth Plateau or Stagnation
Time and again I have heard the argument (mostly from economists) that the US and EU are mature economies and can't expect something like 5% growth. This is absolute rubbish. We are getting more and better tools to increase our growth all the time. Certainly, financial mismanagement such as the Wall St. Panic of 2008 or the coming Euro Crisis can stagnate our economic growth similar to the Great Depression of 1929. But if we intelligently use the tools we have and continue to develop, we can grow vigorously. Let me also add that the EU is not going to grow via 2 hour lunch breaks, 6 weeks of vacation a year or 35 hour work weeks. The EU must be prepared to work....Sorry.

There is another book I recommend reading, "The Great Stagnation". The author is half right and half wrong. Let me start with the half right. He correctly observes that a country is not going to add to its growth by growing the size of government. A lean, mean government is what is needed.

Furthermore, the author is correct in echoing the observations from "Why Europe" in that science/math/experimentation and entrepreneurship are vital for growth. Where the author goes amiss is his judgment that we have picked all the low hanging fruit with regard to science and technology. This is rubbish. It is similar to the pronouncement by the head of the US Patent office around 1900 who said that everything that could be invented had been invented. Then the Wright Brothers flew the first airplane. Oops. The author of The Great Stagnation is obviously not from any technological field. I am.

Steam Engines

One of the critical elements of the Industrial Revolution was the invention and refinement of the steam engine. This gave people the ***power*** to travel by railroad steam engines or steam engine powered ships. These engines provided the ***power*** for British factories. It gave Britain a decisive advantage over other countries. Because of steam, Britain may have had 10 times the energy available as China (on a per capita basis).

An example of what a difference this power could make was illustrated by the 1842 war between Britain and China. How could a small country on the other side of the earth (Britain) using only a few thousand sailors/soldiers bring the mighty Manchus to their knees? It was technology (and good military strategy). The British simply cut the Grand Canal near Shanghai. The Grand Canal was a long canal that was used to bring rice from southern China to Beijing in the north (where they couldn't grow rice). No canal meant no Manchus. It was pretty simple, and steamships were the critical factor.

Computers

Let's leap ahead to the 20th century, and the advent of computers. I went through all my math, physics and engineering courses using a slide rule. On a recent flight from Stockholm to London, I sat next to Dr. O'Reilly from Ireland. He was an aerodynamicist like me, but he didn't even know what a slide rule was. It is a stick with a central part that slides and enables you to perform multiplication, division and other math functions by using logarithmic scales. You can probably find one in a museum. It is better than a pencil and paper, but it is ponderous. I don't even know how to estimate how much more analytical power a computer gives me. Is it 10 times (as with the British-Chinese and steam) or 100 times or 1,000 times or even more. My slide rule was limited to certain math functions. With a computer, I can devise a complete program with many different equations. I can do time consuming multiple regression analysis in seconds. The progress in computer technology has given me and many others a tremendous boost in analytical power. It is like power steering for the brain. It means we can invent many new things relatively quickly.

The nature of technological progress

Sometimes a technical improvement can happen overnight. Generally, however, it is an evolutionary process spanning decades. Let me give some examples from areas I have worked in or been associated with.

Airlines

Lindbergh's flight from New York to Paris in 1927 showed that airline flights would become practical at some time in the future. Amelia Earhart's flights in the 1930s confirmed the same. But it wasn't until the decades after WWII that intercontinental flights really became technically feasible. It wasn't until airline de-regulation in the 1970s that intercontinental flights became both technically and economically viable. That's a 50 year gestation period.

I was part of ushering in the jet age. The DC-8 ground and flight crew shown in the picture below "added more economic value" than all the Derivatives combined (I [16-2] am 5th from right).

MicroChips

The first transistor was built in 1948. It wasn't until a decade later that it was put on a chip. It took several more decades before the first practical personal computers showed up. I can remember getting my first TI-99 computer followed later by my first IBM PC. It was exciting to have a computer in my very own home, but it couldn't be used for too many useful things.....until the internet came along in the 1990s. Interestingly, this was another 50 year gestation period.

Lasers

In the early 1960s, I studied under Dr. Arthur Schalow who was one of the co-inventors of the laser. It was the Cold War, and the Defense Department wanted to turn these lasers into beam weapons to destroy Russian planes and missiles. In fact, as a part of my career I worked on the Airborne Laser Lab in the 1970s. The Defense Department is still pursuing beam weapons today, 50 years later (and getting closer).

After my stint on the Airborne Laser Lab, I switched to the first project on satellite TV. As a part of that project we looked at fiber optics (from the ground antenna to TVs). Fiber optics use laser light in a glass strand. It wasn't practical at the time. Fiber optics only worked if the glass fiber was absolutely straight. The glass fibers couldn't bend and defied interconnection. That was in the 1970s. Today, fiber optical cables can bend and interconnect. The amount of data they can carry is utterly overwhelming. Please read "Telecosm". Fiber optics are at the heart of our powerful worldwide internet system. Who would have believed that lasers would have developed down this path? I was aware of laser technology from the start, and I never would have predicted the success of fiber optics. Technology is just excitingly unpredictable.

Where is technology going?
That's a big question, and I will only attempt a very partial answer. In the book, "Stagnation", the author makes the very valid point that while the internet is wonderful and worldwide, much of it is used for non-productive activities such as Facebook. Agreed. But the potential is much, much more. We are simply at the Lindbergh stage of the internet, Kindles and iPads. Practical use has begun and will blossom more in the future. Let me just take iPads as an example.

Bookmobiles and Libraries
When I was in Franklin grade school in the 1950s, it was a big day when the Bookmobile came by. For those that don't even know what a Bookmobile is (or was), let me explain. Our grade school library was very small. The Bookmobile was a recreational vehicle stuffed with 3 times as many books as our library, and we could check them out for a week. Wow. It was great.

Later when I was in Lincoln Junior High School, I could use the bus to go to our big two room city library. We were lucky enough to have this library in Santa Monica due to a gift by Andrew Carnegie. One room was the reading room with tables and chairs. The other room was the heart of the library – the stacks. There were shelves and shelves packed with books from the floor to the top shelves. I was in heaven. I'll bet that library had 20,000 books.

Today, my Kindle can hold 7,000 books and my iPad can probably hold 20,000. I can (theoretically) hold the old Santa Monica library in my hand. Wow. That's progress. We are on the tip of a **_knowledge revolution_**. How can anyone be pessimistic?

Today only a fraction of the world's books are available electronically, but the number is going up rapidly. In the future, this will undoubtedly include scientific books, papers and theses. Imagine that I was a biotech researcher. If an iPad might hold 20,000 books today, it will hold 200,000 or 2 million sometime in the future (if we can get past the intellectual property issues). As a biotech researcher, I might be able to hold every biotech thesis ever written on my iPad of the future. Would this help me in my research? Absolutely yes. It would be like power steering for my brain. And that is the direction I think we are headed in. We are going to see progress that we simply can't anticipate just as I couldn't anticipate fiber optics.

Synthetic Genomics

Let me give another illustration why I don't believe we have picked all the low hanging science/technology fruit. Craig Ventner has a company in San Diego known as Synthetic Genomics. If the name, Craig Ventner, is not familiar, let me give a brief synopsis of some of the things he has done. He did probably the lion's share of the work in mapping the Human Genome a decade ago. The first time, it took 10 years and $5 Billion to map the billions of genetic letters. Progress has continued. Currently, it takes a day and costs around $5,000.

There is even some talk of it taking minutes and costing $100 in the future.

One of the important issues facing the world today is renewable energy. One way to make gas is from growing algae and separating out the oil. Unfortunately at the present time, it costs about $20/gallon to produce gas in this manner. Generally the approach has been to separate the gas from algae using chemical solvents. However, Synthetic Genomics is using a totally different approach. ***It has altered the genetics of the algae so they secrete the oil.*** Then it is a simple task to separate the oil from the water that the algae is in. It works in the lab. The challenge is to scale it up to an industrial level. BP and Exxon have invested nearly $1 Billion with Synthetic Genomics to do this task.

Per acre, it is possible to get 25 times as much oil from algae as ethanol from corn. Imagine if that $20/gal for algae could be reduced to $3/gal. It would revolutionize the world. If the US grew the same acreage of algae as it does now for ethanol, the US could actually export oil. Furthermore, it would be renewable. Of course, there is no guarantee that oil from algae will be possible at economic prices, but it just might work. If it does, it will show that all the low hanging fruit has not been picked.

Making something out of nothing
Let me make another observation on where technology is going. During the initial Industrial Revolution, it was necessary to have lots of raw materials like coal and iron. However, if we leap ahead to the Computer Revolution, let's

ask what kind of raw materials do we need to manufacture software? My answer is brains + thin air. In short, we are able to produce something of value out of nothing. How can anyone be a pessimist?

Any country, even one with few resources (like Greece), can do this. Israel has fewer resources than Greece but produces a ton more software. If Greece produced as much software as it produces protests, it would be growing. Even tiny Estonia invented Skype.

Exponential Growth

One of the critical aspects of the Computer Revolution was Moore's Law which says that the density of transistors on a chip will double every 2 years. In other words, we will be able to double our computing power every two years and not require additional raw material. Wow. That's the power of exponential growth.

Or, let's consider biotech for a moment. It has the same sort of exponential growth potential. My son, Robert, did some sort of research into E Coli mutant cells. Once he had isolated the desired mutants, he could grow millions of them in a couple of days. Exponential growth!

In short, whether it is software, computers or biotech, it is possible to produce something out of nothing or nearly nothing. A country doesn't have to be lucky like Saudi Arabia or Norway and have oil resources. A country that has nearly nothing can produce quite a bit. Finland, Israel and Taiwan are examples.

Zero-sum or No Limits
I've talked about innovation in computers, software and biotech. If the US develops good data base software, does this mean that Germany can't? Is software development a zero-sum game? Absolutely not. There are no limits to how much software can be developed or which countries can develop it. The same is true for computers and biotech. Or, how about nano technology or robotics? There are no limits. How can anyone be a pessimist?

Ted.com
In the above paragraphs, I have tried to give some ideas of why I am optimistic about the future. But let me refer you to some real professionals – the speakers on Ted Talks. Simply go to www.ted.com. Let me recommend a couple of my favorite talks. The first is by Daniel Kraft (just go to ted.com and search Daniel Kraft and choose "Medicine's Future? There's an app for that.") He combines technology and genetics and extrapolates to the future. Or try Juan Enriquez: Mindboggling Science.

http://www.ted.com/talks/daniel_kraft_medicine_s_future.html

Warning on ted.com. You will not hear anyone extolling the virtues of the 35 hour work week, 2 hour lunch breaks, 6 weeks vacations or bailouts on Ted.com. These people are actually talking about progress and growth. That's the vision that is sadly lacking from virtually all European politicians and economists.

Summary on Growth

In the past 2 Chapters, I have touched lightly on how to create economic growth through "more work" and "more innovation". Sadly, these options are just not being even discussed by the ECB. These concepts just seem to be outside "**The Economist Box**". Some fresh thinking is needed.

The Welfare States of Europe must re-emphasize growth. If they don't, they will turn from Welfare States into welfare states. Their benefits will be less. Perhaps they will even head for Default. Greece is the canary in the mine.

This is a competitive world. Oh, don't worry about US-EU competition. Worry about China. Recently, I was in Narva, Estonia. It had the largest factory in Estonia, the Krenholm textile factory. It dated from the mid-1800s and was even one of the largest factories in Imperial Russia at that time. Last year all 10,000 people [16-3] lost their jobs. It wasn't US manufacturers that put them out of business. It was China. If the EU thinks it can simply tread water economically, the Krenholm story says it can't. China is eating up all the low skill jobs, and the EU had better start innovating again (like Industrial Revolutions 1 & 2).

Economic Truths

More Work = More Growth
More Innovation = More Growth

Part 5. Summary

Chapter 17. Euro Collapse

There are many possible scenarios that will lead to a Euro collapse. In the interest of keeping this book short, I will just present one scenario. Before I discuss that scenario, I will review what happened in the Wall St. Panic of 2008. The Euro collapse scenario will be different, but there are some similarities.

17-1. The Wall St. Panic of 2008 and Economic Collapse

Table 17-1. Wall St. Panic of 2008

1. Trigger – real estate prices go down
2. Subprime Mortgages fail catastrophically
3. Derivatives amplify the Subprime losses
4. Panic amplifies the Subprime losses by a factor of 10
5. Fed quickly exceeds authority in bailout process

The Trigger for the Wall St. Panic of 2008 was a real world problem – a real estate asset bubble. When the prices started coming down in 2007 and 2008, Subprime mortgages started failing at a catastrophic rate. The mortgage failure rate for the time period 2000-2007 was about 1% for normal mortgages and 5% for Subprimes. When prices started falling, the failure rate for Subprimes shot up to 35% for 2007 and my guess is that the cumulative failure rate in 2008 would be closer to 75%. That's catastrophic. Again, as I describe in my previous book, "The Wall St. Panic of 2008", I estimate the total Subprime losses at $400 Billion of which $200 Billion went to Fannie Mae and Freddie Mac while the other $200 Billion went to Wall St. The Fed bailed out Fannie Mae and Freddie Mac to the tune of $180 Billion, but it was not so simple with Wall St.

The $200 Billion loss to Wall St. did transfer to Subprime Derivatives but that was not all that happened. AIG had issued $400 Billion of Credit Default Swaps (many on Subprimes) and was bailed out by the Fed to the tune of $180 Billion. This alone nearly doubled the real world loss on Wall St. Furthermore, there were synthetic Subprime Derivatives of $200 Billion that contributed an estimated $40 Billion loss. Thus Wall St. Derivatives turned a $200 Billion real world loss into $420 Billion.

Wall St. Panic
The truly massive loss was caused by Panic. On Monday September 15, 2008 Lehman filed for bankruptcy. The next day the largest US money market fund announced that it had broken the buck (this means that its assets were less than 100 cents on the dollar; when liquidated it turned out to be 99 cents on the dollar). This created Panic and all money market funds ($Trillions) were suspect. Furthermore, AIG failed and had to be bailed out by the Fed to the tune of $180 Billion. In other words, it took only one day for the situation to turn into a Panic. The Fed had lost all credibility. The Eurozone should bear this in mind. The biggest casualty of the Panic was our stock market which dropped $5 Trillion in value.

Fed exceeds authority
Both prior and subsequent to the Lehman bankruptcy, the Fed performed no analysis of the root problems (including Derivatives). However, subsequent to the Lehman bankruptcy, the Fed did exceed its authority and take immediate steps to

prevent the Panic from turning into a Depression. The Fed guaranteed the assets of all money market funds, and it bailed out AIG which probably prevented further bank failures. The ECB should keep this in mind. It would be better to exceed authority and act promptly to avoid a bad situation turning into a Depression.

Within its authority, the Fed dropped interest rates from 3% to about 0%. This prevented an interest rate spike which would have been disastrous. With interest rates already very low, the ECB will have a tougher time doing this. Second, the Fed assured all banks of liquidity. Again, this was easier for the Fed to do than it will be for the ECB.

17-2. Euro Collapse Scenario
The basic steps are summarized in the Table below:

Table 17-2 Euro Collapse
1. Greece Defaults and Ireland/Portuguese Defaults anticipated
2. Trigger – interest rate spike for European banks
3. Huge Interest Rate Swap Derivative losses due to spike
4. Utter Panic due to double losses (Defaults + Derivatives)
5. ECB prints money
6. Germany leaves the devalued Euro

If it remains true to form, the ECB will keep denying that Greece will default until the day it actually does. At that point, the ECB will have lost all credibility. The Mean Bond Market will take over. These investors will say a Greek Default could cost European banks $500 Billion and Irish and Portuguese

Defaults could bring this total to $900 Billion (It doesn't matter that Ireland and Portugal will not default on the same day as Greece. The perception will be that they will.) The EuroTARP fund had $1,000 Billion to begin with, but it has used $343 Billion for the first round PIG bailouts and has only $657 Billion left. That's not enough to cover the $900 Billion of PIG Defaults. Furthermore, what if Spain needs a bailout?

The Mean Bond Market will be taking its money out of European bonds and putting it in safer currencies (US Dollar, Japanese Yen, British Pound). Just when the European banks are hit by Default losses and need money the most, the money will disappear. In order to attract some money back, the European banks will have to offer higher and higher interest rates. This will be similar to the Greek bonds which started at 3% interest rates and continually rose to 28% interest over a period of a year. European interest rates may not rise to 20%, but it is a virtual certainty that they won't remain at 3%. My estimate is that there will be at least a 5% interest rise beyond the normal fluctuation range and that this will result in a $1 Trillion loss to European banks. The interest rate rise and losses could easily be more.

Since the ECB shows no indication of understanding Derivatives any better than the Fed, it will be at a complete loss when it is confronted with double losses (Defaults + Derivatives). The EuroTARP fund ($657 Billion remaining) will not be sufficient to handle the approximately $2 Trillion in losses ($900 Billion in Defaults and $1 Trillion in Derivatives).

Example: French Bank A

French Bank A has a $1 Trillion Balance Sheet which means it has $1 Trillion in assets. While most European banks are only capitalized to 3% of assets, French Bank A has a healthy 10% capitalization or $100 Billion in capital. Unfortunately, Bank A also has Greek bonds and suffers a $50 Billion default loss on them. Furthermore, it hold $Trillions of Derivatives that do not show up on its Balance Sheets. Large banks typically hold $20-40 Trillion*. It suffers an initial $60 Billion in Interest Rate Swap losses due to the first interest rate spike. Since its $100 Billion in capital will be overwhelmed by its $110 Billion loss, it will go bankrupt if it is not bailed out by the ECB. To make a bad situation even worse, the stock value of the bank will fall in half which will cut its capital in half to $50 Bil. If it goes bankrupt, Bank A's bonds could fail which would cause further losses to other entities as was the case with Lehman.

*For example, when it failed Lehman had $600 Bil in assets and whopping $39 Trillion in Derivatives.

This hypothetical example of French Bank A will be repeated many times if both Default and Derivative losses occur as I anticipate. Bank A's disaster will be repeated throughout the Eurozone to other banks.

Note: Recently, I have started seeing estimates of what Eurozone banks hold in Greek Debt. These numbers are smaller than the above example. It really doesn't matter. There is $900 Bil of PIG Debt out there, and the Eurozone holds most of it. Which banks or which financial entities hold it is secondary.

Utter Panic

In Part 2 (Defaults) and Part 3 (Derivatives), I have tried to paint a very simple picture (Magic + 1) of what is likely to happen. I have very simply defined the losses as Defaults and Interest Rate Swap Derivatives. The reality will be much worse. Just take Derivatives as an example. There are approximately $50 Trillion of Currency Swaps and $30 Trillion of Credit Default Swaps. There will be huge losses in both of these areas. For example, say French Bank A held a substantial amount of Currency Swaps betting on a strong Euro vs. the Dollar. When the Euro tanks (I expect the Euro to fall to 1 to 1 with the Dollar or perhaps even 75 cents to the Dollar), its losses will increase above the Default and Interest Rate Swap losses. Furthermore, the value of its stock will drop towards zero decreasing its capital as happened with Lehman. Short sellers will step in to short its stock making matters even worse. I could go on.

Probable ECB reaction – Print Money

The ECB will realize that it can't let French Bank A or other Eurozone banks fail. Remember the Lehman mistake. Initially, they will be able to use the remaining funds of EuroTARP. However, they will run through those funds relatively quickly. The only alternative open to them (I will suggest another alternative choice in the next Chapter) will be to print money. Essentially this will devalue the Euro and increase inflation.

Germany prints money in 1923

Everyone should read about the hyperinflation in Germany when it simply printed money in 1923. Sources include: Wikipedia: "Hyperinflation in the Weimar Republic", "Hitler's Banker", "Lords of Finance". Essentially, a loaf of bread ended up costing $100 Bil in Deutschmarks. One observer said that there was a straight line between the hyperinflation in 1923 and Hitler in 1932. In short, Germany is very, very concerned with inflation.

Germany will leave the Euro

When the ECB starts printing massive amounts of money, the Germans will simply leave the Euro. The Germans have seen the inflation movie before. They will have no part of it. They will go back to the Deutschmark. ***Without Germany, the Euro will collapse.*** Each country will go back to its individual currency. It will be an absolute disaster. The Euro glue that is such an important part of holding Europe together will be lost.

Summary

Remember, I am an optimist. Although after reading this Chapter, you will think otherwise. A Greek Default will trigger a Panic and huge interest rate spikes in the Eurozone. These interest rate spikes will in turn cause huge losses in the $100 Tril of Interest Rate Swaps which I estimate are held by European banks and other institutions. The combination of Default + Derivative losses will swamp the EuroTARP fund, and the ECB will print money. Germany will leave the Euro, and the Euro will collapse.

> "For want of a shoe a horse was lost. For want of a horse a knight was lost. For want of a knight a battle was lost. For want of a battle a Kingdom was lost. All for want of a shoe."
>
> "For want of a **controlled** Greek Default, the Euro could be lost."

How can a Greek Default be controlled? Next Chapter.

Addendum – For the Skeptics of Derivative Losses

I am predicting both Default and Derivative losses. Some might be skeptical of my predictions on Derivative losses. They might point to the fact that there has been no meltdown in the $400 Trillion Interest Rate Swap market for a decade. Therefore it is safe. For these skeptics I have a two word answer: Subprimes and Madoff.

Subprime Derivatives

Subprime Derivatives have been around since 2000. There was no Subprime Derivative meltdown between 2000-2007. Therefore, one could incorrectly conclude that they were safe. However, a more astute observer would have said that Subprimes hadn't been tested except under benign market conditions with the real estate market consistently going up each year. As soon as the market turned in later 2007, Subprimes and their Derivatives started failing left and right. The trigger for Subprime failure (i.e., a real estate market decreasing in value) was the key.

Madoff

One could use the time test with Madoff as well. For 20 years, his customers never thought they lost a dime. For the SEC, which is incapable of analysis, Madoff looked pretty good too. It took Mr. Markopolos ("No One Would Listen") to "*analyze*" the Madoff situation. He knew Madoff couldn't walk on water. He was right. If the SEC had rigorously obtained the information that Markopolos had to estimate with his Ball Park thinking, the SEC could have nailed Madoff. Instead it took the stock market fall of 2008 to undo Madoff. Oh, Mr. Madoff didn't lose in the stock market because he never put the money there in the first place. What undid him was that his customers had to cover their stock market losses and had to withdraw money from their "safe" Madoff funds. That collapsed the Ponzi scheme (i.e., was the Madoff trigger).

Chapter 18. How to save the Euro

The answer of how to save the Euro in one sentence is: Gather data, analyze it and plan a response to anticipated problems before they overwhelm you. The buck [18-1] stops with the ECB. They are the ones responsible.

Step 1. Gather Data

The ECB should know exactly how much Greek and other PIG debt each Eurozone bank holds. The ECB should know exactly what Derivatives each Eurozone bank holds. The ECB should know exactly how much Interest Rate Swaps (variable end) each bank holds. The ECB should know exactly what the amount capital held by every Eurozone bank. The ECB should know when the Greeks are going to run through their bailout money.

Step 2. ECB Analysis

If we have learned one thing from the European bank stress tests conducted by the European Banking Authority (EBA), it is that they do not know the first thing about analysis (or probably about data gathering). The fact that the EBA is a total loser does not make the ECB a winner but rather the last hope.

The ECB has to take the data enumerated above and analyze it for potential failures such as:

- The PIGs default on 100% of their debt, 60% of their debt. What is the effect on Eurozone banks? Are there sufficient EuroTARP funds to keep these banks solvent.

- If interest rates spike 5%, what will be the losses on Interest Rate Swaps for Eurozone banks? If interest rates spike 10%, what will be the losses?
- What will be the effect of depositor runs on banks?
- What will be the effect of short selling on Eurozone bank stocks?
- How much money would the ECB have to print to make it likely for the Germans to leave the Euro?

Step 3. Plan a response....ahead of time (fund banks)

If the ECB knows that the Greeks will run out of bailout money by May 1, 2012, should it start working with the Greeks earlier? No. The Greeks can't keep a secret. The second that the ECB starts working with the Greeks, the word of a potential Greek Default will be out on the street, and the financial markets will react in a very ugly manner. What the ECB should do is work secretly with the French and German banks that will be damaged by a Greek Default. It should secretly supply these banks with money prior to the Greek Default.

(Note: there are other Eurozone banks that will be affected as well, but the smaller banks can be helped in realtime if the major French and German banks are solidly taken care of. Contact with all the smaller banks will simply increase the chance of word of an imminent Greek Default getting out.)

Step 4. Plan a response....Suspend Derivative Contracts

I have made a Ball Park estimate that Interest Rate Swap losses could add an additional $1 Trillion in damage to the Eurozone financial sector. This could cause the collapse of the Euro and plunge the Eurozone into a 2nd Great Depression. Is there an alternative? Yes. Suspend Derivative Contracts.

I have state my opinion that most Interest Rate Swap Derivatives are synthetic Derivatives and nothing more than gambling bets. I have even gone out on a limb and suggested that a gambling contract is an invalid business contract. Does that prove conclusively that this is the case? No. I'm not even a lawyer, but I do think it gives some grounds for the ECB to suspend Derivative contracts until a thorough investigation can be completed (in EU time, this would surely be at least a year). This action will prevent immediate, huge Derivative losses and perhaps even eliminate most them in the long run.

Step 5. Suspend Short Selling

In my example with French Bank A, I illustrated how a plunge in the stock price of the bank will simply make the economic damage worse. This happened during the Wall St. Panic of 2008. Short sellers nearly drove Morgan Stanley and Goldman Sachs into bankruptcy by driving down their stock prices and thus their capital. Our incompetent SEC did something competent for once. It suspended short selling. This gave the Fed time to transform these Investment Banks into Regular Banks which the Fed could save (and did save). It will be imperative for the ECB to suspend short selling.

Step 6. Forestall Bank Runs

In a Panic, everyone runs to the bank to withdraw their funds. When everyone does this simultaneously, it will cause the bank to fail. This must be prevented. The ECB must put limits on the amount of money that can be withdrawn.

Step 7. Inhibit the damage of an Interest Rate Spike

In the pre Panic stage of the 2008 Disaster, the Fed completely failed. However, after the Panic took hold, the Fed took some immediate actions. It dropped its interest rates to near zero and offered nearly unlimited liquidity (Step 3) to banks. Since Eurozone interest rates are near zero now, the ECB is going to have less to work with than the Fed did. Nevertheless, it must cut interest rates to near zero.

This is not going to make the interest rates demanded on Eurozone bonds in the secondary market go to zero. These interest rates will spike. That will make it expensive for Eurozone banks to issue new bonds. I estimate this need as about $1 Trillion for the first year. The ECB should be prepared to supply this funding rather than the Mean Bond Market. This will mean that the Germans have to agree to this amount of printing money beforehand.

There is a less expensive way to help the banks, but I am not going to mention it here because the ECB could use it to help Greece, and the best solution for the Euro is that Greece leaves the Eurozone and defaults.

Step 8. Act first and ask permission later

Although the Fed completed failed prior to the Lehman bankruptcy, it did some things right post-Lehman which helped prevent a Panic from turning into a Depression. The Fed guaranteed all money market funds after Reserve Primary, one of the largest, broke the buck. It immediately bailed out AIG. It allowed Morgan Stanley and Goldman Sachs to transform themselves from Investment Banks into Regular Banks. The

Fed had no authority to do any of this. Basically it acted first and asked permission later. On Monday Sept 15, it said it didn't have the authority to save Lehman because it was an Investment Bank. On Tuesday Sept 16, it did save AIG, an insurance company. The Fed clearly had no authority to do anything with an insurance company, but it clearly recognized that on Tuesday Sept 16, the US financial sector was in Panic Mode. The ECB should remember this. It has no authority to suspend Derivative Contracts, short selling or limit withdrawals, but there will come a time when this is the right thing to do. The ECB must act first and ask permission later.

Chapter Summary
To save the Euro from the fallout of a Greek Default (and anticipated Irish and Portuguese Defaults), the ECB should take the actions listed in the Table below:

Table 18-1 ECB Actions to save the Euro
1. Gather data from the banks
2. Analyze this data to figure out the funding required
3. Secretly fund the banks before a Greek Default
4. Suspend Derivative Contracts
5. Suspend Short Selling
6. Control bank withdrawals
7. Inhibit the Interest Rate Spike as much as possible
8. Act first and ask permission later

Book Summary
The ECB knows that Greece and the PIGs are in trouble. What it doesn't realize is that the Euro is in trouble. It must let the

PIGs default and go back to their own currencies. It must concentrate all its resources on saving the Euro. That will be a gigantic job in itself.

If the ECB continues to be as out of touch with reality as it has shown thus far, it will probably preside over the demise of the Euro. It is not simply a question of PIG Defaults. These Defaults will spread losses throughout the Eurozone that will cause Eurozone interest rate spikes. These interest rate spikes will cause huge Interest Rate Swap losses (as well as other Derivative losses). All this bad news will be compounded by Short Sellers and Bank Runs. If the ECB waits to "react", it will be too late. It must "pre-empt".

Lesson for the US
The coming Greek Default is a classic case of a Welfare State promising too much and working too little. The gap between promises and revenue has created large and continuous Budget Deficits. These Budget Deficits have continually added to the National Debt to such a point that they are unsustainable for Greece. With its Default and probable 50% devaluation, its Welfare promises will become "half promises". Greece would have been better off to have promised less and kept its Budget balanced. The US National Debt is at 100% GDP and its Budget Deficits are 10% as far as can be seen. The US is about 4 or 5 years behind Greece and in serious danger of becoming a 2nd Greek Tragedy.

Acronyms

CDO – Collateral Debt Obligation – a type of Derivative
CDS – Credit Default Swaps
ECB – European Central Bank
EBA – European Banking Authority
SEC – the Security Exchange Commission that is our watchdog for stock markets and formerly for investment banks
CFTC – this regulator is in charge of the Commodities and Futures Trading Commission and monitors commodities as well as some Derivatives, perhaps 2% of the total amount of Derivatives. At present, this is the only Derivative monitoring.
FCIC – Financial Crisis Inquiry Commission was set up to examine the reasons for the financial crisis in the US in September 2008
PIG - Portugal, Ireland and Greece
PIIGS – Portugal, Ireland, Italy, Greece, Spain
WAG – This actually a term used in government and business. When you don't have good data, you must make a Wild Guess to start the process. What is the A in WAG? Well, this is book is rated PG so I will let the reader figure that out.

Chapter Notes

1 During WWII, Kermit Glantz served with the 17th Airborne which was disbanded after the war. This picture was taken while he was in the 82nd Airborne. He is top right (silver hair). Kermit is my wife's uncle.

2-1 The particular type of Derivatives that caused AIG losses were Credit Default Swaps. In Chapter 9 of my previous book, "The Wall St. Panic of 2008", I discuss these Derivatives.

2-2 See page 227, Financial Crisis Inquiry Report

2-3 See page 50, Financial Crisis Inquiry Report; see Chap 9 of "The Wall St. Panic of 2008"

2-4 $600 Trillion of Derivatives is document at the Bank of International Settlements website: www.bis.org; go to the Statistics tab, then choose: Semiannual OTC Derivative Statistics at end-Dec 2010; then download number 19: Amount of over-the-counter (OTC) derivatives by risk category and instrument (PDF)

3-1 See **2-4**

6-1 The Greeks received a 110 Bil Euro bailout in the middle of 2010. This is 1.3 x 110 = $143 Bil by my assumed conversion rate. The estimates for the Greek GDP (do a google search or use Wikipedia) are roughly $330 Bil. Estimates for the Greek Budget Deficits appear in newspaper at various levels. My estimate is 14% for 2010 and 10% for the remaining years. With the street protests and declining GDP, it could be worse.

6-2 For the IMF data on Greece see Appendix 4.

7-1 See Wikipedia or do a google search for the National Debts of Greece, Portugal and Ireland. Will they default on 100% of their National Debt or a lesser amount? I give two estimates.

7-2 This $870 Bil figure was from a financial newspaper. If you search the Irish Statistics Office, it looks even worse. The bottomline is that the Irish banking system is way out of whack with its GDP just as Iceland's.

7-3 See Wikipedia for Eurozone GDP

8-1 The ECB has committed to give $343 Bil to the PIGs. I am adding the $500-900 Bil possible Defaults on top of this. Strictly speaking, about half the $343 Bil will probably be in the Defaults. Therefore, am I being too harsh in adding the two numbers together. It's not that simple. It is a cashflow problem. If the ECB gives $343 Bil away and then needs another $500-900 Bil for banks, it will have a larger immediate cashflow problem than its ultimate default loss. But who cares? It is going to be bad in any case.

8-2 Let me point out that European Banks can have both direct and indirect exposure to PIG Defaults. If the Banks have lent to some hedge fund which has purchased Greek Debt, and then the hedge fund defaults, the Bank will lose its loan. This is an example of an indirect loss. Also, the ECB not only has a large amount of Greek Debt, but it also has a large amount of Greek collateral from Greek banks. In other words, the Greek banks can't raise cash so they give the ECB the deed on some Greek property and get Euros in cash. When Greece defaults, of course, the collateral will be worth about half. This is just another way the ECB is maximizing its losses.

10-1 Basically the Subprime loss was $400 Bil. About $200 Bil went to Fannie Mae/Freddie Mac and $200 Bil went to Wall St. The $200 Bil that went to Wall St. grew into a $5 Tril loss in the stock market. It was worse as explained in Chapter 10 of my book, "The Wall St. Panic of 2008".

10-2 See my bibliography: Fatal Risk: A cautionary Tale of AIG's Corporate Suicide. You can also get some skimpy information from AIG website, www.aig.com

11-1 This was the best thing the SEC has done in a decade. They nailed Goldman Sachs for $500 Million.

See www.sec.gov/news/press/2010/2010-59.htm

Or go to www.sec.gov and search Abacus CDO.

11-2 Let me try to explain Synthetic Derivatives another way. They look like business, but they aren't. Imagine that someone tried to sell you the Brooklyn Bridge for $1 Million. It looks like business, but it isn't.

13-1 I'm trying to get the idea across that an upward Interest Rate Spike will cause Interest Rate Swap Losses on a scale that we haven't seen before. The Table and Charts are illustrative and not rigorous. In general, we have seen benign (like less than 2%) interest rate changes for the last decade. The exceptions have been 2001 when 9/11 happened. In 2001, there were far fewer Interest Rate Swaps than the $400 Trillion today. In 2008, the Fed dropped rates down to zero. I am sure this caused some significant Interest Rate Swap Losses. Of course, these numbers were and are SECRET, but TARP money covered all losses. What we haven't seen is a real interest rate spike upward. The inevitable Greek Default will cause this despite ECB efforts to keep interest rates low. When that spike hits, the losses will be horrible. I fear my $1 Trillion estimate will be low.

14-1 See my bibliography: "When Government Fails", M. Baldassare. A quick math check will show that 0.03 x $20 Bil = $600 Million in losses, but the Treasurer was leveraged as well. He maximized the loss.

14-2 Why should the Eurozone banks hold a net position on the Variable End of Interest Rate Swaps? Why not Wall St. banks or Hedge Funds? The reason is that the people that made these Derivatives understand which is the dangerous end. As German Bank IKB scussion.

14-3 See Appendix 6. showed with Abacus, Eurozone banks don't. See Appendix 6 for further discussion.

15-1 Socialism is defined as government ownership of the means of production and distribution. It doesn't say anything about marketing which is one of its major problems.

15-2 I worked 7 days a week as a Real Estate Agent. They weren't all 10 hours/day, but it was definitely 7 days/week.

16-1 Yes, I do realize that Galileo and Leibniz were not British. The British were the key developers of the Industrial Revolution, but many Europeans participated in the overall revolution in thinking.

16-2 A picture of me as a Flight Test Engineer

William Thayer

16-3 Narva has a population of 90,000. If every worker has a family of 4, then 40,000 of the 90,000 people were affected. Time for innovation. All of Europe is being krenholmed. They just haven't figured it out yet.

18-1 Europeans might not know what "the buck" means in this context. It does not mean a dollar. I think it started in our military. If Private ABC did something that required punishment and Sgt XYZ didn't want to be the bad guy, he would "pass the buck" (i.e., pass the responsibility) to the Lieutenant who might pass the buck to the Captain etc. This is why President Truman had a sign on his desk that said, "The Buck stops here." Truman didn't duck responsibility.

Bibliography

"A Demon of our own Design", R. Bookstaber
A good book on Hedge Funds and the crash of 1987.
"A Financial History of Western Europe," C. Kindleberger
Great book by a great writer.
"All About Derivatives", Michael Durbin
A good first primer on Derivatives with formulas.
"A Colossal Failure of Common Sense", L. MacDonald
The failure of Lehman Brothers.
"American Colossus", H. Brands
A great story of American economic growth 1865-1900.
"American Economic History", J. Hughes & L. Cain
A good review of "growth" and "adding economic value".
"An Empire of Wealth", J. Gordon
Excellent book on American economic growth and "adding value".
"Analysis of Derivatives for the CFA Program", D. Chance
A thorough book on Derivatives which misses real world correlation.
"Advantage: How American Innovation...", A. Segal
Amen. Time to emphasize growth and innovation.
"Bust: Greece, the Euro and the Debt Crisis", M. Lynn
A better analysis than the ECB by a college student.
"Capitalism, Socialism and Democracy", Schumpeter
Why Capitalism is best.
"Collateralized Debt Obligations", Lucas et. al.
Detailed discussion of CDO Derivatives. Misses real world correlation.
"Collateralized Debt Obligations", J. Tavakoli
Detailed discussion of CDO Derivatives. Misses real world correlation.
"Credit Derivatives & Synthetic Structures", Tavakoli
Detailed discussion of Credit Derivatives. Misses real world correlation.
"Crapshoot Investing", J. McTague
An excellent rundown on the High Frequency Trading ruining our markets.

"Den of Thieves", J. Stewart
The story of Drexel, Burnham, Lambert and Michael Milken.
"Electronic Exchanges", Gorham and Singh
Good Chapter on Regulation.
"Fatal Risk: A Cautionary Tale of AIG's Corporate Suicide" , R. Boyd
The only book I've found on AIG.
"Fixing Global Finance", M. Wolf
Excellent on Current Account imbalances but misses Derivatives entirely.
"Fool's Gold", Gillian Tett
How Derivatives began with JP Morgan.
"Getting Off Track", J. Taylor
Great on Fed discount rate. Misses Derivatives entirely.
"Guns, Germs, and Steel", J. Diamond
Interesting with some valid observations but weak on technology.
"Hitler's Banker (Schacht)," J. Weitz
The 1923 Hyperinflation in Germany and more.
"House of Cards", William Cohan
The failure of Bear Stearns.
"How Capitalism will save us", S. Forbes
Amen. Written by someone who understands growth.
"In Fed We Trust", David Wessel
The role of the Fed in the 2008 Panic.
"Last Man Standing", D. MacDonald
The story of Jamie Dimon, head of JP Morgan.
"Liar's Poker", M. Lewis
Details how Wall St. Traders view customers as suckers. The author quit when he realized he was adding no value.
"Lords of Finance", L. Ahamed
Excellent book on the 1929 Great Depression.
"Mellon", D. Cannadine
The story of the Mellon bank.
"Memoirs: The Great Depression", H. Hoover
The Great Depression as seen by President Hoover.

"More Money than God: Hedge Funds..", S. Mallaby
A good rundown on how Hedge Funds crashed many currencies.

"Morgan", J. Stouse
The biography of JP Morgan.

"No one would listen", H. Markopolos
How the SEC failed to investigate Madoff despite being warned.

"On the Brink", H. Paulson (Sec of Treasury)
His view of the 2008 Panic. He was no JP Morgan.

"Options for the Stock Investor", James Bittman
Explains how options work. Misses real world correlation.

"Quants", S. Patterson
Excellent book on the computerized trading of Hedge Funds.

"Slapped by the Invisible Hand", G. Gorton
Good detailed on Subprime Mortgage Derivatives. Misses correlation.

"Start-up Nation", D. Senor
How a small nation is growing through innovation.

"Subprime Mortgage Credit Derivatives", Goodman
Good study of Subprime Derivatives through 2007. Misses correlation.

"The Ascent of Money", N. Ferguson
A review of finance from ancient times until now.

"The Big Short", M. Lewis
How Paulson and others used CDS on securities they didn't own.

"The Comeback", G. Shapiro
Growth and innovation. Amen.

"The Dawes Plan", R. Dawes
The first American attempt to help the Europeans financially after WWI.

"The End of Wall St.", R. Lowenstein
Very good book on the 2008 Panic.

"The Euro", D. Marsh
A good description of the origins of the Euro.

"The Financial Crisis Inquiry Report", FCIC Report
A good report. The Minority Report shows Derivative ignorance.

"The Great Crash 1929", J. Galbraith
A good summary of the elements of the Great Depression.

"The Great Stagnation", T. Cowen
Valid points especially for Europe, but wrong on science/technology.

"The Greatest Trade Ever", Gregory Zuckerman
Describes how J. Paulson made $20 Billion with CDS.

"The House of Morgan", R. Chernow
A history of the JP Morgan bank from its origins.

"The House of Rothschild Vol 1 and Vol 2", N. Ferguson
The history of the Rothschild banking empire.

"The Housing Boom", Thomas Sowell
Describes the Subprime Mortgage disaster.

"The Imminent Crisis: Greek Debt and the Collapse of the European Monetary Union", G. Wonders
This book predicted the Greek bailout before it happened and anticipates a Euro collapse. Not if the ECB follows my advice or takes similar action.

"The Last Partnerships", Charles Geisst
Describes when Investment Banks actually did investing.

"The New American Economy", B. Bartlett
Good history of Keynsian and Supply Side Economics. Advocates VAT.

"The Road to Serfdom", F. Hayek
Why Capitalism is best.

"The Smartest Guys in the Room", B. McLean
The fall of Enron due to accounting tricks and more.

"The Two Trillion Dollar Meltdown", C. Morris
Good book on the Panic.

"The Wall St. Panic of 2008", W. Thayer
Available on amazon.com and other retailers. This book is in general agreement with the FCIC Report but was written 6 months earlier.

"The Wealth of Nations", Adam Smith
Classic book on Capitalism.

"The World in Depression 1929-39, C. Kindleberger
Classic book on the Depression.

"This Time is Different", Reinhart & Rogoff
Eight centuries of financial meltdowns.

"Too Big to Fail", Andrew Sorkin

Good book on the Panic.

"Too Good to be True", E. Arvedlund

The story of the Madoff Ponzi Scheme.

"When Genius Failed", R. Lowenstein

The story of the LTCM hedge fund failure in 1998.

"When Government Fails", M. Baldassare

The story of the Orange County, Calif bankruptcy.

"Where Good Ideas Come From", S. Johnson

A moderately good book on a tough subject.

"Why Europe", J. Goldstone

Excellent book on why Europe triumphed economically.
(inquiry, science, math, experimentation, entrepeneurship).
It was not "pie dividing". It was growth and innovation.

"Why Iceland", A Jonsson

How Iceland came to default through its wild banks.

"Why the West Rules—for Now", I. Morris

Could be right unless we re-emphasize our growth virtues.

"13 Bankers", S. Johnson and J. Kwak

Very good book details the change from banking to trading and the growth
of the largest banks.

"$1,000 Genome", K. Davies

One scientific/technological growth area as an example.

DVDs

"The Warning", www.pbs.org

The story of how Brooksley Born tried to regulate Derivatives.

"Thinking About Capitalism", J. Muller

Excellent lectures on capitalism.

"Meaning from Data: Statistics made clear", Starbird

Good primer on statistics.

Websites

www.Wikpedia.com
www.google.com

www.federalreserve.gov
www.bloomberg.com
www.businessweek.com
www.wsj.com (Wall St. Journal)
www.ft.com (Financial Times)
www.imf.org (International Monetary Fund)
www.ted.com (search, "Juan Enriquez shares mindboggling science")
www.bis.org (Bank of International Settlements)
www.bis.org/statistics/derstats.htm, press PDF for size of Derivative market

Appendix for Chapter 1. Comparison with FCIC Report

Six months after I published my book, "The Wall St. Panic of 2008", the Financial Crisis Inquiry Commission (FCIC) published its report which essentially came to the same conclusions I did. My book identified 4 major elements: Bad Input: Subprimes, Causes: (1) Leverage, (2) Derivatives and (3) Credit Default Swaps. I also wrote Chapters on the response of the Federal Reserve as well as the role of other regulatory and self-regulatory organizations. Let me briefly compare the FCIC conclusions with my book:

(1) We conclude this crisis was avoidable.
My book describes the avoidable leverage and Derivatives that amplified a Subprime real estate bubble.

(2)   We conclude widespread failures in financial regulation and supervision proved devastating to the stability of the nation's financial markets.
This is covered in Chapters 11 and 12 of my book.

(3) We conclude dramatic failures of corporate governance and risk management at many systemically important financial institutions were a key cause of this crisis.
My Chapters on Leverage and Derivatives cover this.

(4)   We conclude a combination of excessive borrowing, risk investments, lack of transparency put the financial system on a collision course with crisis.
My Chapters on Leverage and Opaque Derivatives cover this.

(5) We conclude the government was ill prepared for the crisis, and its response added to the uncertainty and panic in the financial markets.
This understatement is covered in my Chapters 11 and 12.

(6) We conclude there was a systemic breakdown in accountability and ethics.
My Chapters 12 and 14 cover this.

(7)   We conclude collapsing mortgage-lending standards and the mortgage securitization pipeline lit and spread the flame of contagion and crisis.
My Chapter 6 deals with this.

(8) We conclude over-the-counter derivatives contributed significantly to this crisis.
My Chapters 8 and 9 cover this.   Derivatives amplified an already bad Subprime problem.

(9) We conclude the failures of credit rating agencies were essential cogs in the wheel of financial destruction.
My Chapter 12 and Appendices 6 and 7 deal with this.

In short, my one person effort came to the same essential conclusions as the FCIC. They sliced the pie differently than I did, but all the elements of the pie were the same.   Most people simply stand in awe of the complex financial sector.   How can one person analyze it if the 21,000 person Federal Reserve has problems?   The true answer is that you and I can figure out what is going on if we make the effort to gather data and analyze it.

Appendix 2. Secondary Market for Bonds

In Chapter 3, I mentioned that the Mean Bond Market was demanding 20% on Greek bonds in the Secondary Market. What is the Secondary Market?

Primary Market
When bonds are first issued, this is described as the Primary Market. For example, in 2004, Greece might have issued in a $1 Mil bond that paid 3% interest each year or $30,000 per year. (i.e., 0.03 x $1 Mil = $30,000)

Secondary Market
When the 2004 Greek bond described above is resold in 2011, it is described as being sold in the Secondary Market. Basically, the Secondary Market is any sale after the initial issue of the bond.

How does the Secondary Bond Market work?
If you bought a house in California for $400,000 and sold it in 2011, you might get a price of $300,000. In other words, your house dropped in price by 25%. The change is expressed in price. With bonds, it is expressed in interest rates (bond dealers like to confuse the innocent).

In Chapter 3, I said that the Mean Bond Market was demanding 20% interest rates for Greek bonds. In other words, the Mean Bond Market will only pay a price so low for the $1 Million 2004 Greek bond described above that it yields a 20% interest rate. This is illustrated below:

Originally in 2004
0.03 x $1 million = $30,000
Mean Bond Market demands 20% interest in 2011
0.20 x $ 150,00 = $30,000

In other words, by asking for 20% interest, the Mean Bond Market is saying that it is only willing to pay $150,000 for a $1 Mil Greek bond. It's really more complicated than this because of maturity date, but you get the idea. The Mean Bond Market is saying that Greek Bonds are nearly valueless. (Note: Bringing in maturity date and present value is beyond the scope of this book. I realize that the above example is a perpetuity.)

Appendix 3. Advanced Death Spiral

Let's start with the familiar Table 5-2.

Table 5-2. Death Spiral (Budget Deficit only)			
.	(1)	(2)	
Year	Beginning Nat Debt	Budget Deficit	Ending Nat Debt
2010	100	10	110
2011	110	10	120
2012	120	10	130
2013	130	10	140
2014	140	10	150
2015	150	10	**160**Death Zone

Table 4-1 is very simple and does not include bond rollover. Since I am assuming a Budget Deficit of $10 Bil each year, I will assume a Bond Rollover of $15 Bil which totals $25 Bil. I am going to assume that the country in question must pay 20% interest on the combined Budget Deficit and Bond Rollover. Thus for 2010, country PIG must pay 0.2 x $25 Bil = $5 Bil in interest. It gets worse in 2011 because the Budget Deficits and Bond Rollovers are cumulative as shown in the Table below. The Cumulative Total increases from 25 to 50 in 2011 because it is the sum of the Budget Deficits and Bond Rollovers for both 2010 + 2011.

Table showing interest payments at 20% interest			
Year	Budget Deficit	Bond Rollover	Cumulative Total	Interest Amount
2010	10	15	25	5
2011	10	15	50	10
2012	10	15	75	15

If I add in these additional interest payments to Table 5-2, the net result is to move the Death Zone up to 2012 from 2015. Higher interest is deadly.

Please compare the Table below to the first Table shown in this Appendix. The Death Zone comes sooner because of higher interest rates.

Table	Showing how 20% interest rates moves Death Zone sooner			
.	(1)	(2)	(3)	
Year	Beginning Nat Debt	Budget Deficit	Higher Interest	Ending Nat Debt
2010	100	10	5	115
2011	115	10	10	135
2012	135	10	15	**160 **Death Zone****

If I repeat the same Table with the interest rate at a mere 10% instead of 20%, the results are not much better.

Table	Showing how 10% interest rates moves Death Zone sooner			
.	(1)	(2)	(3)	
Year	Beginning Nat Debt	Budget Deficit	Higher Interest	Ending Nat Debt
2010	100	10	2.5	112.5
2011	112.5	10	5	127.5
2012	127.5	10	7.5	145.0
2013	145.0	10	10	**165.0 **Death Zone***

Higher National Debt leads to higher interest rates which speed up the trip to the Death Zone. Greece will never be able to return to the Mean Bond Market with its high National Debt. Greece is toast.

Lesson for the US
In 2009 and 2010, the US ran 10% budget deficits and 10% deficits are predicted for 2011 and 2012. This is financial suicide. Greece will be the first suicide victim. The US should be paying attention.

Appendix 4. IMF data on Greek Default

I get the data I use for estimating Greece's Budget Deficits and Bond Re-Financing Requirements from a variety of sources including newspaper, magazines and websites. Naturally these data are more accurate for historical data (e.g., the year 2010 which has occurred) and less accurate for their projections forward (e.g., years 2011 and 2012). What I do is take these data and the credibility of the sources (a subjective judgment, of course) and come up with my weighted average number. Consequently I cannot point to a single source for my data (which means this book probably won't be approved for a PhD thesis).

Let me give an example using data from the International Monetary Fund, www.imf.org. If you access this site and search for "Greek Bond Rollover Requirement", it will come up with a list of articles. About halfway down the page is one entitled, "Greece: Third Review Under the Stand-By Arrangement.....".   Go to Table A1. "Greece: Public Sector Debt Sustainability Framework". In general the data in the Table are given in terms of percent GDP (presumably the Greek GDP).

Let's look at my Table 5-1. "Greek Death Spiral". In 2013, I assert that the Greek National Debt will be $529 Bil or 160% GDP. Now look at the IMF Table A1 and observe the top line "Baseline: Public sector debt 1/". Look at the number for year 2013. It is 158% GDP which compares pretty favorable with my estimate of 160% GDP.

Let's look at my Table 5-2 "How long does the Bailout Fund last?". I start out with $143 Bil of bailout funds and keep subtracting my estimate for yearly budget deficits and yearly bond rollovers. At the end of 2012, my number is -53 which means the Greeks have used up all their bailout funds and are $53 Bil in the hole. The IMF doesn't present their data in this manner, but you can deduce pretty much the same result from what they do present.

In the middle of the Table A1, there is a line that says:

	2010	2011	2012	2013
"Gross financing need 7/ In billions of US Dollars"	62.8	69.5	77.5	76.7
My alteration	31.4	69.5	77.5	
Cumulative alteration	31.4	100.9	178.4	

Note: 143 – 178.4 = -35.4 Bil

What I did to make the IMF data closer to my format is to take the financing need for 2010 and divide it in 2 because the bailout started in the middle of 2010. That's called "My alteration". Then I simply added the needs up in a cumulative manner (i.e., cumulative for 2011 is 31. 4 + 69.5 = 100.9, cum for 2012 = 31.4 + 69.5 + 77.5 = 178.4). At the bottom, I merely subtracted the cumulative sum of 178.4 from the bailout funds of $143 Bil which yields a negative $35.4 Bil. That means Greece is short $35 Bil at the end of 2012. This means it will run out of money part way through 2012. Please note that my estimate in Table 5-2 for year 2012 is a negative $53 Billion vs. the IMF's negative $35 Bil. Now the IMF and I may be off in our estimates, but at least we are in the same Ball Park. What I am suggesting is this. The IMF may not be coming out and explicitly saying that Greece is going to run through its bailout money by 2012, but a careful reading of its report certainly suggests that this is what is going to happen.

My suggestion to the IMF is that run another line in their report which compares cumulative financing need with the bailout funds available like my Table 5-2. My suggestion to the ECB is that they read both this book, and the above IMF Report.

Appendix 5. Saving Greece

Let me simplify the math in order to outline my solution. I will assume that
the Greek GDP is $300 Bil (vs. $330 Bil). I will assume that government
spending is half the GDP or $150 Bil (typical for a Welfare State). Since
the Greeks have a $30 Bil deficit, this means their tax revenue is $120 Bil.
The Greeks have two problems:

(1) They must pay $30 Bil for their budget deficit
(2) They must rollover $40 Bil of their $430 Bil National Debt each year

They need an additional $70 Bil in tax revenue.

VAT Plan
VAT is value added tax and is approximately 25%. I will first assume for
simplicity that is a 25% tax on everything in the GDP (this is definitely on
the high side). Thus it generates 0.25 x $300 Bil = $75 Bil of the $120 Bil
tax revenue. If the Greeks need $70 Bil more, they just need to raise their
VAT from 25% to 50%. This would enable them to pay their deficit and
pay down their National Debt at $40 Bil per year.

The reality is that the VAT is probably on something like 50% of the GDP
so the Greeks would have raise the VAT from 25% to 75% which would
effectively make everything about 50% more expensive. I think that is a
pretty fair estimate of where the Greeks are -- between a rock and a hard
spot. The likelihood is that they will get to the same position by leaving the
Euro and going back to a devalued Drachma.

More Work Plan
Everyone is suggesting more cuts in expenses for the Greeks, but no one is
suggesting "more work". Let me. If the Greeks simply cut their 6 week
vacations to an American size 2 weeks and worked 4 hours on Saturday,
they could meet both their deficit and rollover financing (360 more
hours/year). This would be 20% GDP increase (in theory), and I
conveniently assume that all this extra growth would go to the government.
Furthermore, I assume the Greeks could find something productive to work
on (i.e., ignore the marketing problem).

143

Appendix 6. Subprime and Interest Rate Swap Triggers

Subprime Trigger
First, let me refer you to my previous book, "The Wall St. Panic of 2008", which goes into much more detail than I will do here.

The bulk of the Subprime Mortgages were made to people with Subprime credit ratings (which turned out to be accurate) and who put no money down. They also paid low, below market interest rates for the first 2 year period. In other words, if the true interest rate that they would have to pay was 8% because they were Subprime, they would actually be able to get a mortgage at 4% for the first two years.   Then their mortgage payments would double at the start of year 3 to 8%. These loans were called 2/28 loans (2 years at low interest and 28 years at high interest). However, the housing market prices were going up at 10% per year. If they bought a house for $200,000, it would be $240,000 by the time their 2 year period of low interest was up, and they could re-finance with a new 2/28 loan. Great plan. It worked while the market went up, and then the real estate prices started coming down. Now at the end of their 2 year period, their house had actually dropped 20% in value and was worth $160,000. There was no way they could re-finance their mortgage (not enough equity), and they couldn't afford a doubling of their mortgage payments. They defaulted. My estimate is over 75% of them defaulted.

If an observer had reviewed Subprime Mortgages from 2000-2007 and seen a 5% failure rate, he would say that they were basically OK. But the US real estate market was rising every year from 2000-2007. Before the observer said Subprimes were OK, he should have waited to observe them during a real estate downturn. When the real estate prices started down in 2007-2008, the Subprimes just fell out of the sky. Message: Before pronouncing a Derivative as sound, it should be put through a stress test and that test will vary depending upon the type of Derivative.

Subprime Trigger
A real estate market that finally went down in price after 10 years of going up was the trigger for Subprime Derivative failures.

Interest Rate Swaps

Interest Rate Swaps have been around from 2000 to 2011 and have not failed. Does this mean they are safe? No. They just haven't been put through their stress test. Interest rates have roughly been 3% + or − 2% for the 2000-2011 period. This is not a huge variation. Interest rates can spike upward or downward. When they are at 3%, it is pretty hard to spike very far downward. However, how far can they spike upward? There is no limit, and an upward spike in interest rates is the real stress test for Interest Rate Swaps.

Greek bonds were issued at a 3% interest rate for most of the 2000-2010 period. However, once it became apparent that the size of their National Debt and Budget Deficit had been greatly understated, their interest rates spiked to 20%. After the 1st Eurozone bailout, their rates dropped down towards 10%, but subsequently they have risen back to 20% (and 28% at the time of this writing). This rise from 3% to 20% in a period of a year is what I define as an interest rate spike.

Size of the Interest Rate Swap market affecting the Eurozone

There are two numbers which will determine the size of the Interest Rate Swap loss for the Eurozone banks. The first is the size of the Interest Rate Swaps (the variable end) held by Eurozone banks. The second is the size of the interest rate spike affecting these Swaps. Perfect knowledge of these two numbers would allow an easy calculation of the loss. For example, if the Interest Rate Swaps held were $100 Trillion and the interest rate spike was 5%, then the loss would be a staggering $5 Trillion.

The total worldwide market for Interest Rate Swaps is $400 Trillion. If I say Europe has half, this is $200 Trillion. To be conservative, I will say that the Eurozone has only $100 Trillion (since it is only a portion of the European market). If interest rates have been spiking a maximum of 2% during the 2000-2011 period, then the worst case would be 2% x $100 Trillion or a $2 Trillion loss. We haven't seen this. Why?

Hedging your bets

If I think the Steelers are going to win the Superbowl and bet $100, I might start getting nervous if I hear that the quarterback has a sore elbow. I might decide to hedge my bet by making a $50 bet on the Packers. Sure, I will only win a max of $50 now, but it will also cut my max losses to $50. I suspect that this type of activity is happening in the Interest Rate Swap market. In the best case, the cross betting or cross buying could reduce the net Interest Rate Swaps from $100 Trillion to $20 Trillion, the size of the European bond market. If this were the case, then a 2% spike would result in a loss of 2% x $20 Trillion = $400 Billion. That's large but manageable with an estimated $800 Billion in capital for European banks. Also, it has been rare during the 2000-2011 time period, that interest rates have changed 2% in a single year. The biggest change was in 2001 when Interest Rate Swaps were not the huge market that they are today. The big change in 2008 was covered by TARP money.

Empirical Data
Throughout the period 2000-2011, we have not seen crippling losses in the Interest Rate Swaps market. Probably this means that yearly net losses have been somewhere in the $200-$400 Billion range. This means that my model of an effective size of the Eurozone Interest Rate Swap market of $20 Trillion is probably in the ballpark. Let me assume for the moment that this is true. Then I have half the data I need for my estimate of Interest Rate Swap loss. The loss will be $20 Trillion x ? interest rate spike.

Estimating the size of an interest rate spike
Who knows what it will be. In the secondary bond market, we have Greek bonds spiking from 3% to 20%, Portuguese bonds spiking from 3% to 10% and similar numbers for Irish bonds. There will probably be a number of different European interest rates involved. It may be interest rates for a particular bank or an index based on a country or region. It is tough to estimate one average interest rate spike for all of these. However, I will. Interest Rates have been roughly 3% + or -2% for roughly a decade. With the Default crisis, I think that interest rates will spike 5% above this range. If you review European interest rates around the 1990 time period, there was much turmoil without any Defaults. This could be a rough guide to what will happen this time around. If you look at British interest rates in 1988-89, there was a spike of 6% in a one year period, and the British rates are relatively stable. No Default was involved. It is an estimate, of course, but I will predict at least a 5% interest rate spike above the normal

fluctuations we have seen from 2000-2011. I used 7% in my Table and Figure which would be a net 5% above a nominal 2% fluctuation.

Estimate of Interest Rate Spike Losses for Eurozone Banks

My estimate is that Eurozone banks will be holding a net $20 Trillion of the variable end of Interest Rate Swaps that will suffer a 5% interest rate spike. Therefore the losses will be 5% x $20 Trillion = $1 Trillion.

Interest Rate Swap Trigger
A spike in interest rates (e.g., 5% above the normal fluctuation range) will cause massive losses to the holders of the variable end of Interest Rate Swaps.

Is this any kind of scientific proof that the Eurozone banks are heading for a $1 Trillion loss due to Interest Rate Swaps? Of course not. I am making an estimate. My point is not to get a number that is exactly right, but to estimate a number in the ball park. I think that $Trillions in losses is the right ball park. It is going to be much more than mere $Billion or even hundreds of $Billions.

The Subprime Derivative market was a mere $2 Trillion which resulted in a $400 Billion loss. The total Interest Rate Swap market is $400 Trillion. Even if I reduce this to $100 Trillion for the Eurozone and reduce it even further to $20 Trillion of net Interest Rate Swaps, this is still gigantic when compared to the Subprime Derivative market. If a relatively small $2 Trillion Subprime market can bring the American economy to its knees, what can a $20 Trillion net Interest Rate Swap market do to the Eurozone economies? It could cause a Euro Collapse and Eurozone Depression. Please look at the Figures on the next page for a visual comparison of the sizes of the Derivatives markets involved.

Comparison of the relevant Derivative Sizes

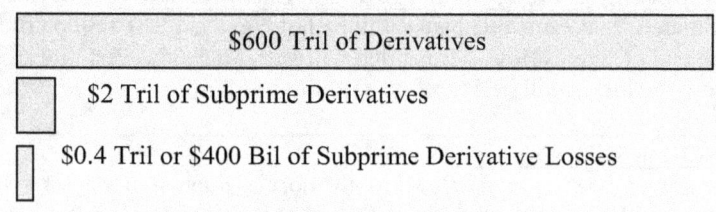

Figure   2008 Subprime Crisis

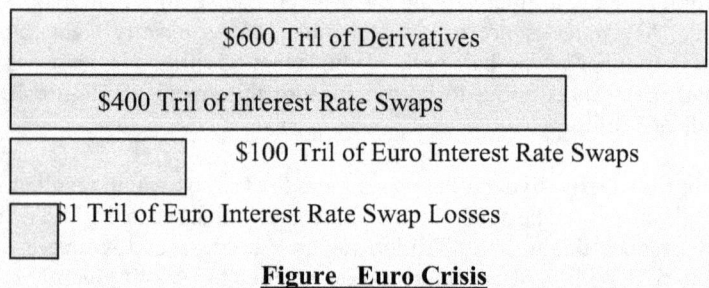

Figure   Euro Crisis